GERMANY IN UNIFORM

**DAS HEER, DIE KRIEGSMARINE, DIE LUFTWAFFE,
THE POLICE, THE NATIONAL SOCIALIST PARTY, THE RED CROSS**

1933-35

Paul GAUJAC

Translated from the french by Lawrence BROWN

Histoire & Collections

CONTENTS

FOREWORD

December 1933 saw the publication
in Berlin of a uniform guide book showing
not only army and navy uniforms, but also those
used by the various police forces,
state organisations and those, of course,
dependent on the National Socialist Party.

This surviving booklet bears the stamp of the central library of the North Sea naval base. It has 55 pages, 38 of which show in colour, groups of three or four people from the various state or political organisations

These are shown in the following order:

the armed forces – *Reichsheer* and *Reichsmarine*

the police forces of the various German provinces (*Länder*)

the political organisations – SA, SS, etc.

the organisations linked to aviation

the technical and voluntary work organisations

the state and provincial organisations - railways, postal, customs, rivers and forestry.

The accuracy and diversity of the various uniforms shown, as well as the aesthetic value of this booklet make it a very valuable item not only for historians, but also those interested in uniforms. With its diversity of subjects and the undeniable charm of its illustrations, it allows us to glimpse what Germany was like when Hitler took power.

In order to present this subject in light of the years that were to follow, it seemed better to slightly modify the order in which the various organisations were presented. Aviation, therefore, is placed immediately after the navy, and the various services and organisations are then grouped together under the Party banner, something that was the reality in any case, except for state organisations only shown in pictorial fashion; they neither belonged to the armed forces, nor the Nazi Party.

Still with the intention of bring more clarity to the reader's understanding, the two opening chapters cover Hitler's rise to power and the second the transformation of the *Reichswehr* into the *Wehrmacht*, consequence of the material covered in the first chapter. This then takes us to a little more than a year after the publication of this booklet in Germany, whereas the formation of armoured forces, the main component of the future German conquests, is seen a little later.

Indeed, with such a subject it is impossible to pause at a precise moment as one could do with a photograph. The evolution of the various organisations was dictated by their own rules and by the attention or interest that its leaders held for them. Thus, the turning point for the army was in 1932, whereas that of the navy and the SA was in 1934.

The same seemed necessary to complete the original charts with texts that showed the changes and characteristics of the various elements of the arms of service covered in this book. This has been carried out by using period documents (texts and photographs), notably those published by the French 2nd bureau intelligence services that were particularly well-informed about the growing strength of German armed forces.

As for the German terminology, they have been mostly translated and accompanied, when necessary, by the original word. This is not always easy to do, notably for the ranks and echelons, especially for the Party organisations. Thus, in some cases, the German terminology has been retained.

We might venture to say.

Firstly, it became clear when reading period documents that all Germans felt a desire for revenge and that consequently the actions of the successive leadership of the nation was a result of the Versailles *Diktat* and the failure of the Republic, leading to rise of Nazism.

Also, the militarisation of state organisations and the

Sturmabteilungen members at the shooting range.

amount of Party paramilitary units gives one the impression that all Germans wore a uniform.

For the Germans, already fond of military uniforms, this tendency would increase throughout the following years, to such an extent that when the French entered southern Germany, they discovered that even men who had lost their sight during the war had their own distinctive attire.

Next, by looking at the abundance of military, state and political organisations, we discover that the German people were placed in an order of battle, controlled by an increasingly powerful army, a more and more efficient police force on a national level, and a political party that infiltrated institutions and indoctrinated the young.

Finally, it is obvious that German rearmament had never ceased, even during the Weimar Republic, and that Hitler and the Wehrmacht were in this case the direct heirs. We also discover that plans elaborated before rising to power and of which some were applied immediately after, too time to implement. This was notably the case for the armies in need of materiel and, therefore, dependent on industry, such as the navy and air force or men trained for service with the army.

In 1939, the *Wehrmacht* was still growing and the generals hesitated, therefore, to engage it too early in a war. But Hitler decided otherwise and sadly, what followed meant that he was right, at least for a while.

ADOLF HITLER AND HIS RISE TO POWER, 1929-34

Born from the aftermath of the Great War, the National Socialist Party slowly merged with Germany itself. Its history followed exactly the various political stages of Adolf Hitler's political career, with the latter eventually holding all the power in 1934.

ADOLF HITLER AND THE NATIONAL SOCIALIST PARTY

Having joined the *Deutsche Arbeiter-Partei* on 16 September 1919, Hitler became its propaganda chief in January 1920. The party then changed its name to *Nationalsozialistiche Deutsche Arbeiterpartei* (NSDAP) (German national socialist workers party), adopting the swastika symbol and with Hitler taking over the leadership on 29 July 1921.

As it was initially almost entirely made up of veterans, the NSDAP was the direct heir of Prussian military traditions, working firstly for German unity, then later, German expansion.

From the very moment the party was formed its stated aims were:

-to complete the German unity started by Bismarck, following the methods of the latter, eg. *fire and iron* [1]

-to avenge the Versailles *'Diktat'*;

-to create Greater Germany (*Grossdeutschland*) as outlined by the Frankfurt parliament in 1849 and revived by Wilhelm II in the shape of Mitteleuropa

-to revive the concept of Pan-Germanism of the imperial period, reincarnated in a mystical idea of a predestined people, a chosen people superior to all other races and called upon, thanks to its cult of a warrior's sense of honour, to regenerate the world.

For Hitler and the Party, these four objectives would be achieved by a 'Prussianisation' of Germany and the transformation of the German nation into an instrument of war.

The Party was a corporate public law body and a living entity whose role was to give the state its vital impulse. The close coordination between its services and the public authorities would be maintained on all levels by a unified personnel.

At the beginning, for straightforward reasons of timing, the Party and the army were present within the state with their own structures. Indeed, it was imperative to hide the rapid rebirth of the German army from the victors of 1918. However, as soon as circumstances allowed for it, the mask was dropped.

Hitler himself defined their relationship in unequivocal terms:

"The Party gives the people to the army the people, and the people give the soldiers to the army, but in this way, both provide the German empire with the security of peace at home and the strength to assert itself."

Until 1933, Germany only had an official army reduced by the Treaty of Versailles to the symbolic number of 100,000 men. This was the *Reichswehr*, an army with many officers of aristocratic origins created by the law of 23 March 1921. There was, however, a second working class brown shirt army. These two armies were united by the same ideal, the same ardent desire for revenge and to recommence, when the time was right, the pursuit of the Pan-Germanist program.

HITLER AND THE NSDAP'S STRUGGLE FOR POWER

In July 1929, Alfred Hugenberg, president of the nationalist conservative party, opposed the Young Plan that was established to settle the problem of German reparations imposed after the Great War and formally adopted a month later at the Hague conference. However, while the conservatives had everything at their disposal except the masses, the Nazis had everything at their disposal except money. Supported by the Steel Helmet (*Stahlhelm*) paramilitary organisation that was openly opposed to the politics of the Weimar Republic [2], the NSDAP launched during the summer a referendum against the adoption of the plan and asked Hitler to lend his support. With each bearing in mind their mutual needs, an agreement was reached between the two parties. However, Hitler, making the most of the nationalist party's means of communication, spread Nazi ideas throughout the country. The referendum only garnered six million votes, but

Adolf Hitler at the time of the Munich putsch. *(Private Collection, All Rights Reserved)*

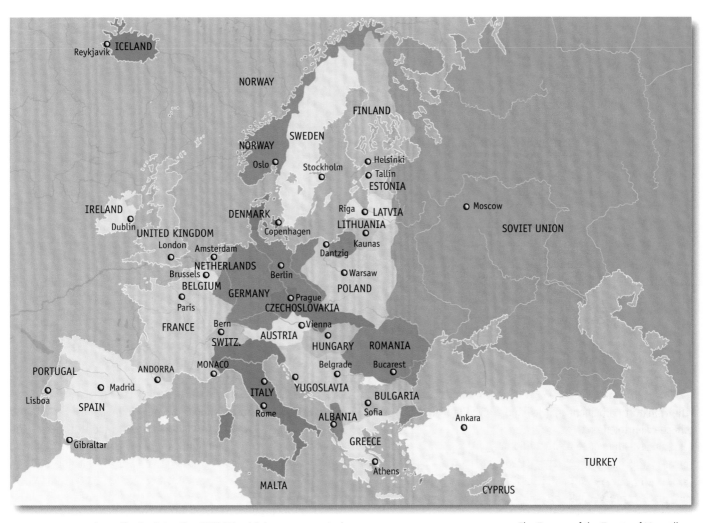

The Europe of the Treaty of Versailles.

many new members flocked to the NSDAP which now counted 176,500 members at the end of the year.

New Reichstag elections were held on 14 November 1930 and the Nazi Party obtained 107 seats with six and a half million votes.

On 10 October 1931, Hitler had his first meeting with Reich president Field Marshal Hindenburg [3]. The results of this meeting were negative and Hitler accepted an alliance with the Parti Deutsch-National and *Stahlhelm*. By the end of the year, the Party had 806,000 members.

Hindenburg's mandate expired in 1932 and Hitler decided, on 22 February, to put himself forward as a candidate for the presidency of the Reich. Four days later, the Nazi government of Brunswick named him as government councillor, thus conferring him with German nationality.

After the first round of voting on 13 March, Hitler obtained 11 million votes (30%), whereas Hindenburg had 18 million (50%). The government made the most of this advantage to carry out searches in the NSDAP offices and close all of the Party's troop meeting places: storm detachment (*Sturmabteilungen* or SA) protection squads (*Schutzstaffeln* or SS). Despite this, the Party retained its fighting spirit and, at the second round of voting, obtained 37% of the votes.

Frightened by the growing number of Nazi Party members, the government took measures to attempt to eliminate it. On 13 April 1932, a decree promulgated the immediate disbanding of the SA

1. *By iron and fire.*
2. Also called *Bund der Frontsoldaten* (League of Frontline soldiers) founded at the end of 1918 at Magdeburg gathering together Great War veterans frustrated by the defeat of 1918 and the later humiliating measures imposed by the Treaty of Versailles. It was the largest paramilitary organisation in Germany with 500,000 members in 1930.
3. *Feldmarschall* Paul von Beneckendorff und Hindenburg, President of the German Reich and Supreme Commander of the Armed Forces.

Arbeiterpartei Adolf Hitler leaves one of the first propaganda meetings organised by the *Nationalsozialistiche Deutsche*.

and SS. However, on 12 May, General Wilhelm Gröner, minister of defence in disagreement with the army, was forced to resign, followed by Chancellor Brüning fifteen days later.

The government then formed by Franz von Papen was a 'presidential cabinet' that relied exclusively on Hindenburg's approval. It would try, not to block the progress of National-Socialism, but to integrate it, or as some said, 'disband' it in all spheres of German political life. Upon Hitler's request, the government took two measures that were favourable to the Nazi Party: the *Reichstag* was dissolved on 4 June and the decrees and ministerial orders forbidding the SA and SS to wear uniforms and carry out public demonstrations were cancelled.

The elections that took place on 31 July 1932 were once again a success for the NSDAP, which obtained 230 seats, thus becoming the most powerful party that Germany had ever seen. However, president Hindenburg refused to allow Hitler, the *'Bohemian corporal'*, to form a new cabinet. The only position offered to Hitler was that of vice-chancellor, and he declined this offer.

A struggle now took place between the NSDAP and the von Papen government that was supported by the Deutsch-National conservative party. Finally, the Nazis gained the upper hand thanks to Hermann Goering who succeeded on 12 September in obtaining a *Reichstag* score of 513 ballots against 32 for a vote of no confidence concerning the cabinet. The assembly was dissolved immediately afterwards.

The Nazi Party now leaned increasingly towards the working classes and intervened vigorously on their behalf, particularly during a public transport strike.

More moderate elements were frightened by the demagogic violence of Goebbels' speeches, and factory owners withdrew their financial support from the Party, losing votes in the elections of 6 November 1932, in whichit obtained only 196 seats and lost two million votes. But von Papen did not have the majority of the Reichstag and refused to look for support from the workers' unions. He was forced, therefore, on 17 November, to offer his resignation.

Hindenburg then asked Hitler to form a new government based on parliamentary majority, but without changing the situation created by von Papen in Prussia where the Reich had taken in hand the administration and the Prussian police [4]. The negotiations failed, and on 1 December 1932, General Kurt von Schleicher, minister of defence since May, was placed at the head of the government. Von Schleicher then tried to reduce Hitler's influence within the National Socialist Party by giving the offices of Vice Chancellor and Prime Minister of Prussia to Gregor Strasser, head of the first organisation section of the NSDAP.

Strasser's defection threatened the Party with internal scission. To avoid this, it was imperative to quickly annihilate Strassers' influence with the northern German sections and calm down certain Nazi members of parliament who feared losing their mandates, and resolve the financial problems.

On 8 December, the first organisation section was disbanded and the following day, Hitler gathered together all his leaders and Nazi members of parliament in order to obtain their adherence. By 30 December, the crisis was over and Strasser found himself totally isolated.

---

4. He suspended the Prussian government, resigned by 'mutual agreement' and replaced it with a Reich commissary.

ADOLF HITLER'S TRIUMPH WITH THE SUPPORT OF THE ARMY

On 3 January 1933, Field Marshal Hindenburg named Adolf Hitler as Chancellor of a coalition government and ordered the *Reichswehr* to cooperate with the new regime. Hitler then held talks with von Papen the following day in order to finish with von Schleicher who, after much intriguing, was forced to hand in his resignation on 28 January.

After fourteen years of effort, the National Socialist Party was at last in power. In this new government where von Papen was Vice-Chancellor, there were only two other national socialist ministers alongside Hitler: Goering as commissionaire for aviation and home office minister for Prussia, and Dr Frick, the Reich home office minister. Hitler, however, would make the most of the situation to develop the influence of the NSDAP and take all of the power. Supported by right-wing parties, he obtained, on 1 February, the

dissolving of the *Reichstag* and on the 7th, the same for the Prussian Landtag.

Goering began combing out the upper echelons of the police administration in order to replace them with SA and SS members. He then turned on the Communist Party that was suspected of plotting an uprising; its press was banned and the Red Front disbanded. In the elections of 5 March 1933 no mandates were awarded to the communists as their party had been declared illegal. The NSDAP obtained 288 *Reichstag* seats.

In addition, the southern German states protested against the decree *'For the protection of the people and the state'* issued by Hindenburg that allowed the Chancellor to not only act against the excesses of political parties, but also against any form of insubordi-

The German Länder in 1933.

A. Anhalt
BR. Brunswick
OLD. Oldenburg
BP. Bavarian-Palatinat
PR Prussia
STR. Strelitz
TH. Thuringen

nation on the part of the provincial governments (*Land*). The threat of a monarchist and regional putsch seemed imminent and on 8-9 March, Dr Frick took control of the police in Württemberg, Bavaria and Saxony. Despite the orders issued by the Bavarian government, the Bavarian police did not react, and on 10 March von Epp formed a new ministry with Ernst Röhm and Heinrich Himmler. The same day saw the forming of national socialist governments in the southern provinces and, a few days later, in Hesse.

The National-Socialist Party had triumphed, and on 27 March Hitler obtained from the *Reichstag* full powers for a four-year period.

On 11 April, sailing from Kiel to Königsberg on board the pocket battleship *Deutschland* on the eve of the spring manoeuvres, Hitler and General Werner von Blomberg, Minister of Defence, along with General Werner von Fritsch and Admiral Erich Raeder, Commanders-in-Chief of the army and navy, looked at, the possible successors to Hindenburg. The following day, Hitler and von Blomberg looked at how this could be done. Von Blomberg gave his word that he would support Hitler with all his power in the looming battle for the succession of the Reich presidency and promised to use all his influence with the military powers to obtain their support. As for Hitler, he declared himself ready to put an end to the intolerable ambitions of Röhm and his SA to form a people's army, and ensure that the *Reichswehr* would be the only entity to deal with questions of a military order.

As for homeland matters, Hitler's goal was to unify all of the national formations and to leave only one party remaining, the NSDAP. Once these goals had been achieved, he passed a law on

14 July 1933 forbidding the creation of new parties. Then, on 1 December, the '*Law to safeguard the unity of Party and State*' declared that the NSDAP was itself the incarnation of the State. When the was renewed on 12 December, there was a list formed entirely of Nazis who thus formed the government with a total of 661 members of parliament.

However, the SA general staff, commanded by Röhm, wanted to see the assault divisions transformed into a national army commanded by SA leaders. But the *Reichswehr* opposed this vehemently. Röhm then attempted to lead the SA into a second revolution and entered into open conflict with Hitler. He was encouraged by the former Chancellor von Schleicher and even by von Papen.

Hitler decided, on 30 June 1934, to act first. Backed by the SS, commanded by Heinrich Himmler, as well as Goering and all the SA leaders that had remained loyal to him, he put down any opposition in a bloodbath: Röhm, forty-nine SA leaders, Strasser, von Schleicher and several figures close to von Papen were executed. Hitler then took control of the SA and began their reorganisation.

Upon Hindenburg's death on 1 August 1934, the German government decided to confer upon Chancellor Adolf Hitler all the prerogatives of president. On the 19th, Hitler received 88% of the total votes cast. He became Reichsführer and Chancellor and Supreme Commander of the Armed Forces, whilst the NSDAP now incarnated the German nation.

State funeral of Field Marshal von Hindenburg on the site commemorating the battle of Tannenberg.

CHRONOLOGY

9 November 1918. Proclamation of the German republic.

16 November. Creation of the German Officer League (*Deutscher Offiziersbund*).

28 December. Creation of the National Association of German officers (*Nationalverband deutscher Offizier*).

19 January 1919. Edict relating to the reorganisation of the *Reichswehr*.

28 June. Signature of the Treaty of Versailles.

5 July. *Generalleutnant* Hans von Seeckt is named as head of the *Truppenamt* of the Ministry of Defence, head of the *Reichswehr* reorganisation committee.

20 January 1920. The Treaty of Versailles comes into force. Article 160: '*The Army shall be devoted exclusively to the maintenance of*

order within the territory and to the control of the frontiers.'

1920-34 President of the Reich and Supreme Commander. Reich Chancellor, Minister of Defence, Chief of the Army and Navy High Command.

1 June. *Generalleutnant* Hans von Seeckt, commander of *der Heeresleitung*, the equivalent of Army Commander-in-Chief.

Generalmajor Wilhelm Heye, head of the *Truppenamt* of the Ministry of Defence.

1 January 1921. Foundation of the army (*Reichsministerium*/head of *Heeresleitung* Nr 1240/20 Stab): '*Formation of the army is completed. A new chapter in the history of the German army begins.*'(von Seeckt).

23 March. Law on the organisation of the *Reichswehr*.

1923. *Generalleutnant* Otto Hasse, head of the *Truppenamt* of the Ministry of Defence.

11 January 1923. Occupation of the Ruhr by the Allies.

26 April 1925. *Feldmarschall* Paul von Beneckendorff und von Hindenburg is elected President of the German Reich and Supreme Commander of Armed Forces.

1925. *Generalleutnant* Wetzell, head of the *Truppenamt* of the Ministry of Defence.

4 September 1926. Germany becomes a member of the League of Nations.

7 October. *General* Hans von Seeckt resigns. *Generalleutnant* Wikhelm Heye, becomes head of *Heeresleitung*.

16 December. Intervention by Scheidemann at the *Reichstag* concerning clandestine rearmament.

31 January 1927. Departure of the Allied Control Commission.

30 January 1928. *Generalmajor* Wilhelm Groener, Minister of Defence.

1 October. Admiral Erich Raeder,

Commander-in-Chief of the *Reichsmarine*.

1 October 1929. *Generalleutnant* Baron Kurt von Hammerstein-Equord, head of the *Truppenamt* of the Ministry of Defence.

December. The end of the Allied withdrawal from the Ruhr.

1 November 1930. *Generalleutnant* von Hammerstein, Commander-in-Chief of the Army.

Generalleutnant Wilhelm Adam, head of the *Truppenamt* of the Ministry of Defence.

10 April 1932. Field Marshal von Hindenburg is re-elected President of the Reich.

13 April. Decree promulgating the disbanding of the SA and SS.

13 May. Resignation of *General* Groener.

30 May. Franz von Papen replaces Brüning as Chancellor. *General der Infanterie* Kurt von Schleicher, Minister of Defence.

16 June - 9 July. Lausanne Conference: the end of reparation payments.
17 June. The decree concerning the SA-SS is cancelled.
20 July. Von Papen removes the Prussian government and places Prussia under the authority of a *Reich* commissar.
31 July. General elections: 130 Nazi members of parliament at the *Reichstag*.
5 August. Meeting between Schleicher and Hitler at the Fürstenberg barracks.
17 November. Von Papen resigns.
3 December. *General* von Schleicher Chancellor and Minister of Defence.
28 January 1933. Resignation of von Schleicher.
30 January. Hitler Chancellor of a national coalition government. Hindenburg orders the *Reichswehr* to cooperate with the new regime.

31 January. Hitler's speech to the Berlin garrison.
General der Infanterie Werner von Blomberg, Minister of Defence.
27 February. The *Reichstag* fire.
5 March. General elections: 288 Nazi members of parliament at the *Reichstag* (340/647 to the coalition)
4 April. Creation of a Reich defence council.
1 July. Hitler defines the relationship between the SA, Stahlhelm and the *Reichswehr*.
1933. General der Artillerie Ludwig Beck, head of the Truppenamt of the Ministry of Defence.
14 October. Germany retires from the League of Nations and the disarmament conference.
1 February 1934. Generalleutnant Werner Freiherr von Fritsch, Commander-in-Chief of the Army.
12 April. Hitler-von Blomberg-von

Fritsch conference on board the *Deutschland* concerning the future relationship between the army and the SA and the consequences on the hypothetical death of Hindenburg.
30 June. "Night of the long knives".
2 August. Death of Field Marshal Hindenburg. Adolf Hitler becomes Führer and Chancellor of Germany.
9 March 1935. The creation of the Luftwaffe is officially announced.
16 March. Law on the construction of German armed forces. Obligatory national service is reinstated.
Creation of a new army totally freed from the "*Diktat*".
21 May. New law concerning the *Wehrmacht* and secret defence.
July. Law concerning the defence of the Reich: the *Reichswehr* becomes the *Wehrmacht* and the *Heer* is created. The remaining manpower is

recruited.
1935. *Generaloberst* Ludwig Beck, Commander-in-Chief of the Army.
7 March 1936. Occupation of the demilitarised Rhineland zone.
General von Blomberg is promoted *Feldmarschall*.
Admiral Erich Raeder is *named Generaladmiral* and Commander-in-Chief of the *Kriegsmarine*.
1934-38 The *Führer* and Chancellor. Supreme Commander of Armed Forces.
Ministry of War (*Reichskriegsministerium*) Commander-in-Chief (*Oberbefehlshaber der Wehrmacht*)
General von Blomberg; Commanders-in-Chief of the Army, Navy and Air Force: *Oberbefehlshaber des Heeres: General* Beck
Oberbefehlshaber der Kriegsmarine: Admiral Raeder; *Oberbefehlshaber der Luftwaffe*: General Goering.

FROM THE REICHSWEHR TO THE WEHRMACHT, 1929-35

In Germany prior to 1914, the army held a very important position within its institutions and was held in great esteem by the nation. Indeed, a Rhineland proverb states, *'Der Mensch beginnt mit dem Leutnant'* .
It was also the tradition for military personnel, even if their rak was a low as 2nd class private, to be placed in the front row during public or high society events.

Despite appearances, the German defeat of 1918 did not in any way mark a gap in the history of the German army. Although it was reduced by the 1919 Treaty of Versailles, it remained for Ger-

many, a country undergoing rapid political, social and economic changes, the framework of the state, the symbol of unity and the incarnation of the *Deutschtum* with its vague and indistinct bor-

During the 5 May 1935 ceremonies on the *Königsplatz* in Berlin, the new *Wehrmacht* constitutes the honour guard of the regimental emblems of the old imperial guard.

ders, representing the notion of fatherland for the German people.

It was within and around the army that the idea of revenge was first fomented, before crystallising into the desire for power and conquest of National Socialist Germany.

FROM THE TEMPORARY *REICHSWEHR* TO THE PROFESSIONAL *REICHSWEHR*

Following the defeat, the Weimar Republic retained an army formed from the ruins of the imperial army. This *'temporary Reichswehr'* of 300,000 men was essentially a law and order force and a counter-revolutionary militia. It constituted, however, an important step towards unification by removing the four contingents of the confederate states. The head of state was the supreme leader, but it was to the constitution and not the head himself that its members had to pledge allegiance.

Thereby a German national army emerged, dependent on a sole government, that of Berlin, thus achieving military unity.

The same time saw the creation, immediately after the Armistice was signed in 1918, of two organisations, unknown to the government, but kept secret by the Ministry of Defence of the time, and whose influence was decisive and objectives crystal clear. The 'League of German officers (*Deutscher Offiziersbund*) created in November had the objective of *'keeping intact all the forces necessary to the rebirth of the nation and a guarantee for the moulding of the youth.'* As for the 'National League of German officers' (*Nationalverband deutscher Offizier*) created a few days later, it saw itself as

COMMAND AND SERVICE FLAGS
1. Black-white-red flag
2. President of the *Reich*
3. Service of the *Reich*
4. *Swastika* flag
5. *Reich* post
6. Former naval officer serving as a merchant ship captain
7. *Reich* Minister for Defence
8. *Reich* war flag

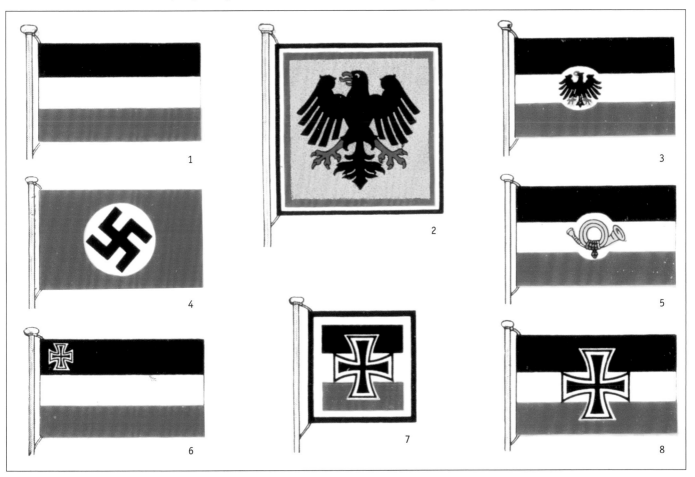

'a combatant political organisation and a 'shock troop' for national defence and the monarchy'.

Also, in January 1919, the Weimar Republic appealed for volunteers wishing 'to take part in the defence of the Fatherland's borders and interior law and order'. Following this official recognition, the numerous, already formed 'Free Corps' (Freikorps), turbulent and troublemaking at times, would soon become a ready made mass of manpower to support the ambitions of the nationalists and directly serve the designs of the military.

It was in this somewhat agitated climate that the new German army saw the day and began to be constituted in 1921. After several warnings from the victors, the Weimar Republic was forced with an obvious lack of good will to resign itself to apply the clauses of the Treaty of Versailles. The 'temporary Reichswehr' of 300,000 men, of which 40,000 were officers, thus ceded its place on 1 January 1921, to a 'professional Reichswehr' reduced in size by two-thirds. Added to this was also the disbanding of the supreme general staff and the Kriegsakademie. An army recruited from voluntary enlistment and with officers chosen amongst the best combatants of the last war, it presented itself as both the continuation of Bismarck's ideals and as a new step in the standardization and organisation of the German army. By its very composition, it was an army of officers and

During exercises, infantrymen armed with a light MG 34 defend their position against the advance of the 'enemy'.

1. General in mess uniform
2. Staff Lieutenant-colonel in field uniform
3. Major in mess uniform (infantry)
4. Captain in field uniform with greatcoat (infantry)

It was ready to play the role that it had been cast in *General* von Seeckt, a general of the old army and Commander-in-Chief of the Army in March 1920:

1. To uphold Prussian military tradition.

2. To circumvent the clauses of the Treaty of Versailles.

The creation of the *Truppenamt*, a camouflaged resurrection of the disbanded general staff, and the nomination of General von Seeckt following his intervention of the von Kapp monarchist putsch in Saxony clearly adhered to this dual objective.

For von Seeckt, the *Reichswehr* had to remain in close touch with the entire population and be intimately linked to the nation. With national service no longer in vigour, 'tradition companies' were placed in every regiment to retain the flags of disbanded corps. Also, it was declared that 'these companies must maintain close contact with veterans' associations. It would be better if the recruits were garrisoned in the regions they come from in order to retain links with their families, their villages or towns'.

The *Reichswehr*, which according to von Seeckt 'is above parties', thus became an officer and NCO army that would not have any problem in assimilating recruits as soon as obligatory military service was brought back.

According to the clauses of the Treaty of Versailles, the army was not allowed to have any heavy armaments such as tanks, anti-tank weapons, artillery, anti-aircraft guns or aircraft. All manufacture of such weaponry was forbidden and any material left over after the Armistice had to be handed over to the Allies, although some did escape from the investigations carried out by the Inter-Allied Control Commission. The constraints of the Treaty were, therefore, circumvented in the great tradition of Prussian renewal that took place after the defeat of Iena in 1806, by using subterfuge, notably by masking the names of units and materiel that they were equipped with, and by testing new equipment in the USSR.

NCOs and an army of revenge that foreshadowed the future national army (*Wehrmacht*).

THE NEW REICHSWEHR

The *Reichswehr* of 1921 grouped together both the *Reichsheer* (ground forces) and the *Reichsmarine* (navy).

Limited to 100,000 men by the "Diktat" of Versailles, the *Reichsheer* comprised 4,000 officers and 96,000 NCOs and men, forming seven infantry and three cavalry divisions commanded by two *Gruppen-Kommandos*. Recruitment was on a voluntary basis with twelve years service for other ranks and twenty-five for officers.

This aristocratic army, in a typical Frederick the Great style, with its traditional regiments of the imperial army and garrisoned in the same towns, was recruited not from bottom to top, as was the case with the temporary *Reichswehr*, but from top to bottom, beginning with the general staff and ending with the other ranks.

Very soon, with the consent of the Ministry of Defence, field artillery batteries were transformed into anti-aircraft units, and some new materiel was put into service. Above all, beginning in 1921, technical studies were undertaken for the manufacture of modern weapons such as planes, tanks and combat gas. The USSR helped Germany by placing at its disposal experimentation centres and training grounds. In exchange, it received officers and NCOs for the training of its own army. This military collaboration, which began in 1921 upon the instigation of von Seeckt, came to an end in 1933 for two reasons:

-political relations were strained between the new German government and the Soviet Union

-Germany deemed itself authorised to continue testing on its own soil, as opposed to expansive foreign ground.

The strength of the navy, limited to 15,000 men, of which 1,500 were officers, was not enough to arm all the units conceded by the Treaty: forty ships. It was strictly forbidden to have submarines and an air arm. Looked upon with suspicion by conservative circles after the 1917-18 mutinies and by the left-wing parties following the failed far-right von Kapp putsch, the navy was totally cut off from the nation. Therefore, it immediately adopted a revisionist stance and set itself the goal of equalling the French navy.

Under the impulse of Admiral Wegener, its renewal was undertaken in conformity with the clauses of the Treaty. From 1921 to 1928, three light cruisers and twelve 800- tonne destroyers were successively laid down. Also, in 1928, it was decided to build the Deutschland battleship as a replacement to the old *Schlesien* class cruisers.

THE TURNING POINT OF THE 1930S

Change arrived in 1930. Three years before Hitler took power, the Reich government, acting on the initiative of Chancellor Brüning and no longer only the *Reichswehr*, defined a large rearmament program and the establishment of an army much larger than that stipulated by the Treaty. The disappearance of the Inter-Allied Control Commission and the early withdrawal of the left bank of the Rhine were the reasons for these changes.

With Chancellor Brüning's propositions rejected at the 1932 Geneva disarmament conference, the military authorities, with the full agreement of the political powers, came up with a total overhaul plan that was to be undertaken by 1938. The *Reichswehr* proper remained a professional army supplied with recruits serving for three years. It would be completed by a militia

of equivalent strength founded on a three-month period of service followed by short training periods.

By the end of these reforms, the *Reichsheer* was to comprise 300,000 men forming twenty-one divisions. The 'Umbau' rearmament plan also foresaw the creation of armoured and aerial units. As for the Kriegsmarine, and still with the aim of parity with France, the program planned for a 'balanced strength' according to the designs of Admiral Erich Raeder, the navy commander since 1928, notably including six or eight battleships and three aircraft-carriers. In fact, the initial plan was limited to four 2,200-tonne destroyers.

In 1934, after the departure of Germany from the League of Nations on 14 October of the previous year and faced with the refusal of its request for equal rights at the Geneva disarmament conference, the new regime decreed the creation of an army of 300,000 men serving in the short term. The birth of the latter,

INFANTRY IN FIELD UNIFORM
1. Second-lieutenant
2. Light machine-gunner
3. Skirmisher equipped with a gas mask
4. Light infantryman with gas mask

named *Wehrmacht*, was signed by the decree of 16 March 1935, ordering, in reply to France bringing back two-year military service, obligatory military service for all German men between the age of 18 and 45 in order to form three *Gruppenkommando*, twelve army corps and thirty-six divisions, and the creation of the Luftwaffe. All of the earlier stipulated conditions required for the creation of a large national army were, therefore, united.

The law made it obligatory for men and women, to serve their country in wartime.

The usual cycle of obligation (18 to 45 years of age) could be extended depending on needs and could go as far as total requisition regardless of age or gender.

In peacetime, there were three types of obligatory service:

Active service (*Aktive Dienstpflicht*) being called up at 20 full years of age and with a variable length of service (actually one year by the of 22 May 1935)

Being available for service (*Beurlaubtenstand*)

Landsturm where all men aged over 45 were to serve in wartime. There were three categories of available manpower:

• The *Reserve* where former soldiers were placed at the end of their military service up to the 31st of March of the year they reached 25 years of age.

• The *Ersatz Reserve* comprising men subject to military obligations aged no more than 35 and who would not be called up for active service.

• The *Landwehr* comprising men that could be called up from the 1st of April when they reached 35 years of age to the 31st of March following their 45th birthday.

The new law offered the military command almost unlimited possibilities. With the combination of military service and paramilitary service, and the powers held by the War Ministry in deciding when to call up and train reservists, it could be said that in peacetime, the Reich could put all of its strength on a war footing whenever it needed to. Alongside this army and its caste system was another, more working class and political. The 'brown shirt army' of the National-Socialist Party in fact constituted a danger for the aristocratic flavoured *Reichswehr*, if anything due to its strength of 500,000 well-organised men who underwent military training every Sunday and whose leaders received at least a basic tactical training. Also, the Party's Sturmabteilungen had the support of the Stahlhelm, with the latter having become its first source of reserve manpower, bringing its total strength to more than three million men. The army did not, however, oppose the law on civil service of 7 April 1933 that led to the expulsion of Jews. They also accepted, without the slightest reaction, the symbol of the NSDAP, the eagle with spread wings holding a shield with the swastika in its talons, something that was worn on the headwear and tunics of officers and other ranks. The adoption of the red flag and swastika was not opposed in any way either.

The SA leader Röhm, however, was suspected of using his men to achieve a total overhaul of the army. In doing so, he wanted to become the Minister of Defence and make the SA the militia that the *Reichswehr* wanted for its rearmament. In fact, the two million men thus available would progressively absorb the old professional army, in order to provide the Reich with a great army, if not national, at least one of the people, without having to fall back on military service,

However, the military powers absolutely wanted to:

Retain the 'monopoly of arms' and be the only armed defender of the nation.

Retain or conserve the right to intervene in, or even control, foreign policy if diplomatic action could lead to conflict.

There was also a latent antagonism between the two armies, but

3

4

Mountain light infantrymen in the Bavarian Alps.

forces, I shall render unconditional obedience and that as a brave soldier I shall at all times be prepared to give my life for this oath.'

There was now harmony between the political powers and the army, happy with the measures taken for its rearmament and with its monopoly of arms confirmed. However, although the antagonism with the SA was stifled, at least at the lower echelons, it remained alive in the upper echelons of leadership.

With Hitler having gained power, the political neutrality of the army ceased to be a essential requirement. Many young officers embraced the new theories and most of the elder, higher ranking officers concealed their conservative tendencies; the two trains of thought that were prevalent within the *Wehrmacht* at the time were, therefore, National-Socialism and Prussian tradition:

'*But it should also be noted that certain events, such as the purge of 30 June 1934, have somewhat tempered the initial enthusiasm.*

the National-Socialism's accession to power in March 1933 forced them both to co-habitate despite their reciprocal reticence.

However, Röhm's behaviour worried both Hitler and the military command, and the secret agreement made on the Deutschland in the Baltic Sea led to the 'Night of the long knives' where Röhm was eliminated and the SA brought to heel.

The very next day, General von Blomberg, Minister of Defence, issued an order of the day to the army:

'*The Führer has personally dealt with the mutineers and traitors with a martial decisiveness and exemplary courage... The* Wehrmacht, *the sole armed force in the Reich, remains above the conflicts of interior politics, but once again states its professionalism, devotion to duty and loyalty. The Führer asks us to establish cordial relations with the new SA. We will comply with joy to this demand, convinced of serving in this way a common ideal*'.

THE WEHRMACHT AT THE END OF 1935

On 2 August 1934, officers, other ranks and sailors swore allegiance to Hitler in their barracks and on board warships:

'*I swear by God this sacred oath that to the Leader of the German empire and people, Adolf Hitler, supreme commander of the armed*

MOUNTAIN TROOPS
1. Mountain light infantry
CAVALRY
2. NCO in walking out uniform
3. Trumpeter
4. Cavalryman in field uniform

It has required a minister of national defence to mediate during two years in order for concessions to be made by both parties. Although the uniforms bear the swastika and the army and navy have sworn allegiance to the *Führer*, the SA and SS have been brought to heel. Without trying to foresee what will happen in the future, we can state that the 'Prussian way has won over the other and that, eventually, politics will go the same way.'

Of course, the increase in manpower and the decrease of length of service did not favour the value of small units. But, everything had gone well and the *Reichsheer* had gained more in quantity than what it had lost in quality.

The functioning of its paramilitary institutions and the spirit that animated its youth allowed it to conserve its homogeneity intact whereas, at the same time, it substantially increased its power.

The National-Socialist militias had to finally bend to the rule of the *Reichswehr*, initially jealously guarding its prerogatives, then fearful of the brown shirt army compromising the project of creating a strong and modern army at the service of the nation.

'In the new society that it has created, the regime led by Hitler has given back the army its veritable role, its true colours:

-Within Germany itself by eliminating, on 30 June, the most influential of its political competitors and by raising the army up as the educational guide of German youth

- Abroad, by allowing the army to forge the instrument that will allow it to confront any eventual foreign intervention that its fait accompli *policy could prompt (a hardening of its vengeful attitud, equality in terms of armament, leaving the League of Nations' disarmament conference). In the name of a predestined role that has always led it to believe in its hegemony in Europe, German has regained its armed power, the symbol of its eternal strength.*

What will come of this association of mysticism and cult? 1934 has seen the formation of a new military organisation (the tripling in size of the Reichswehr, creation of new units, increase in man-

The *Gebirgsbrigade* of Garmisch-Partenkirchen was soon equipped with a mountain artillery group.

power, short term service, thorough military training, solid career options, adoption of forbidden modern weaponry). 1935 will no doubt see a clarification. What will be the next stage?'.

Everything was set for the *Wehrmacht* to rapidly develop, notably with the formation of Panzerdivisionen and creation of the Luftwaffe that would make it the most powerful army in the world.

Thus, the regular forces of the *Wehrmacht* remained, the sole defender of the nation (*Waffenträger der Nation*).

In the name of German principles of total war for which the German people had to be prepared without reserve, the leaders of the Reich pursued their efforts that had begun several years earlier. The objective was to place all the armed forces, equipped with the most up to date material (land, air and sea), in the hands of a sole high command.

The law of 16 March 1935 that brought back obligatory military service and established the number of twelve army corps and thirty-six divisions that the army had to rapidly create, rendered official the violation of the Treaty of Versailles, something that had been latent since the beginning of 1934.

The law of 21 May set the organisation of the high command of armed forces and military service for all Germans. It contained the discretionary powers that would allow it, with the unlimited support of the people, to put into place a military program designed by the German leadership and whose main aims were:

-To constitute strong, modern regular armed forces led by a sole high command

-To retain auxiliary armed forces capable at any time of undertaking the role of combatant units

- To Keep paramilitary forces preparing or completing training given by the *Wehrmacht*

-To train the youth militarily

- To rearm and equip the country for a military role.

The law made it obligatory for men and women to place themselves, at the disposal of the Fatherland in wartime. The usual cycle of obligation (18 to 45 years of age) could be extended if need be and could go as far as total requisition whatever the age or gender.

« Infanterie... Marsch! »

DAS HEER

In addition to a centralised Reich, one of the first measures taken by the members of parliament in session at Weimar of 1918 was to provide Germany with an army which, although greatly reduced in size as stipulated by the clauses of the Treaty of Versailles, was more unified in terms of organisation and leadership, something that the imperial army had never been. Indeed, once Bavaria, Saxony, Württemburg and the semi-autonomous state kingdoms had been removed, their own war ministers, general staffs and armies disappeared.

The army and the navy was placed under the authority of the national Ministry of Defence (*Reichswehrminister*), becoming part of the cabinet and with a sole commander-in-chief.

For the first time in its history, the German army found itself with the nomenclature of *Reichswehr*, organised on the lines of a permanent unification that had nothing in common with the temporary unifications that had taken place for the needs of a common cause at the time of the empire.

The downside, however, was that the concessions accepted by the government in order to adhere to the clauses of the Treaty of Versailles meant that it fell out of favour with the army whose strength of 400,000 men was reduced to 100,000, thus throwing the remainder onto the streets, where the depression had already created millions of unemployed.

It was in this poisonous atmosphere of putsches, settling of scores between the various political factions of the Freikorps, attempted provincial rebellions and governmental instability, that the '*temporary Reichswehr*' was first born. It then became a '*professional Reichswehr*' within which the *Reichsheer* acquired the stability necessary to reform a real army that all army generals so ardently desired.

THE *REICHSHEER* FROM 1921 TO 1931

Given that the Treaty of Versailles only authorised 100,000 men, it was only possible to have seven infantry and three cavalry divisions. They were controlled by two *Gruppenkommando*s in Berlin and Kassel where the Staffs played the role of an army general staff.

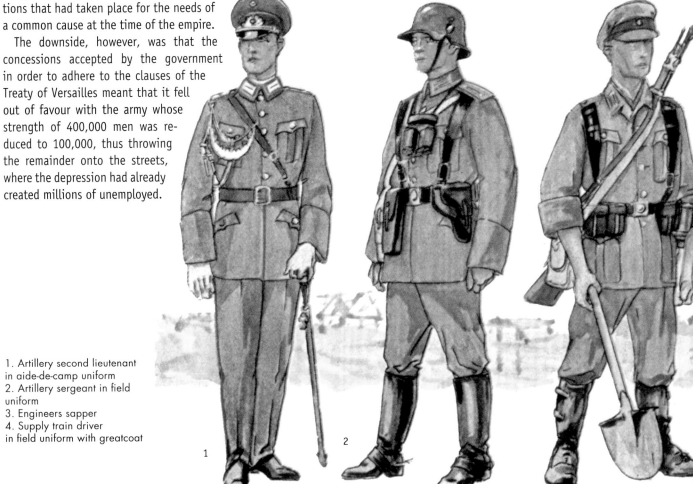

1. Artillery second lieutenant in aide-de-camp uniform
2. Artillery sergeant in field uniform
3. Engineers sapper
4. Supply train driver in field uniform with greatcoat

1

2

The commander of each infantry division also held the command of the territorial region where the divisions were based (Wehrkreis):

- *Gruppenkommando*   Berlin
- 1st Division   *Wehrkreis* I   Eastern Prussia
- 2nd Division   *Wehrkreis* II   Pomerania, Mecklenburg, Schleswig- Holstein
- 3rd Division   *Wehrkreis* III   Silesia, Brandenburg
- 4th Division   *Wehrkreis* IV   Saxony, Prussian Saxony
- *Gruppenkommando* 2   Kassel
- 5th Division   *Wehrkreis* V   Thuringia, Hesse, Württemburg, Baden
- 6th Division   *Wehrkreis* VI   Brunswick, Hanover, Oldenburg, Westphalia
- 7th Division   *Wehrkreis* VII   Bavaria

The 1st and 2nd cavalry divisions were commanded by *Gruppenkommando* 1 and the 3rd by *Gruppenkommando* 2, before being later commanded by a cavalry corps.

Each infantry division comprised:

- An infantry command general staff (*Infanterie-führer*)
- An artillery general staff (*Artillerie-führer*)
- Three infantry regiments and a mortar company
- A three-group artillery regiment
- A squadron attached in peacetime to a cavalry (*Reiter-Regiment*)
- A two-company engineer battalion, a bridging company and searchlight section
- A two-company signals group
- A three-company transport group
- A medical group (attached to a territorial element).

The cavalry divisions comprised:

- Six four-squadron cavalry regiments
- A mounted artillery group (attached to an artillery regiment in peacetime).

For recruit training (*Ausbildung*), there was a specialised battalion in each infantry regiment, a squadron per cavalry regiment and a battery per artillery regiment.

10.5 cm (l.F.H. 16) light field howitzer.

Training courses for the new generation of officers were held at the arm of service schools: infantry in Munich (later in Dresden), cavalry in Hanover, artillery in Jüterbog and engineers in Munich.

The continuity of the imperial army was ensured at the level of the small units by their place of garrison and province of origin.

However, all the projects for development came up against the lack of materiel. Thus, in 1930, when it was envisaged in the event of war to form twenty-one divisions by tripling the strength, the stocks of weapons and munitions only allowed for the equipment of fourteen of them.

It was in these conditions that a second armament program was established in 1932, that wasto extend from 1 April 1933 to 1 April

A telephone line is rapidly rolled out to link the new HQ with the units during an exercise.

7.9 mm (s.M.G. 08) heavy machine-gun in firing position.

1938 and cover the needs of twenty-one mobilised divisions. The budget allocated for this program was 374 million marks, with approximately 110 million secretly taken from the War and Home Office budgets. Although the secret funds remained under the control of the Reichstag budget commission and accounts verification services, the number of people 'in the know' was very small.

This explains why the *Reichswehr* wanted an army of 21 divisions, a more realistic objective than the 36 imposed by Hitler without consulting his generals.

THE TURNING POINT OF 1932-33

The year of 1932 was marked by the intensification of training and the appearance of new equipment.

Undertaken in the most realistic conditions possible, collective training was carried out in the second half of the year during:

- periods spent by troop units in camps
- field exercises for cavalry units and signals detachments
- special technical exercises for engineers and radio and telephone units
- numerous exercises.

Amongst the new equipment we can cite:

- the 7.5 cm gun whose lightness and tactical mobility made it a support weapon for a war of movement
- the 10.5 cm infantry gun
- the all-terrain armoured car and office equipped command car.

INFANTRY AND CAVALRY

Within the infantry, the quest for firepower, flexibility and mobility was seen as being a priority concern. Thus, the three-platoon double rifleman group infantry company, each armed with a light machine-gun, and two or three groups of skirmishers, were replaced by a three-platoon company of three identical groups, each equipped with an automatic weapon. The number of light machine-guns was, therefore, increased by half, with nine now for the new company compared to six for the older format.

Anti-tank defence saw the appearance of a motorised company of six guns at the divisional level. For anti-aircraft defence, trials were being undertaken in order to equip the infantry with an anti-aircraft weapon.

Once it had provided flexibility and mobility, the inherent qualities needed for a war of movement, the aim of the command was to provide the German infantry with the means to allow it, in the event of close-quarter combat, to deal quickly and efficiently with all eventualities.

During the August manoeuvres devoted to the tactical use of combat tanks, and those of September that looked at the composition, armament and command of large cavalry units, the command looked with particular interest at the use of motorised reconnaissance groups and the crossing of river obstacles by large masses of cavalry.

These manoeuvres were an opportunity to experiment with the two-division cavalry corps and organic unit formula. The corps was not reduced, as it had been up to that point, to only coordinate divisions that had been temporarily united. It now had its own breakthrough group with missions taken from the division, that now conferred upon it the aspect of a large, permanent and homogenous unit.

The cavalry division now found itself reduced to four cavalry regiments and four artillery batteries. However, with its reconnaissance unit and its high density of motorisation, it made up with mobility and flexibility for some of the strength it had lost to the cavalry corps. The regiments were constituted with four or five horse squadrons and a technical squadron of which the support artillery was replaced with an anti-tank gun section.

With the added appearance of radio-equipped armoured cars, it was obvious that, like the infantry, the cavalry was being prepared for an important role in battle; Through its own means would have to be able to carry out its role. Admittedly, apart from special experimentation units, no real tank was in service, but it was common

During an exercise, a patrol takes up position along a railway in order to observe the enemy.

A 15 cm (sFH 18 für Kraftzug) heavy field howitzer changes position. The gun is in its road transport configuration.

knowledge that several prototypes of light combat vehicles, known as "*Tankjaeger*", or German or foreign means of manufacture had been tested. Also, some Reichswehr officers and NCOs had taken part in exercises in the USSR involving combat tanks in action. Comprising of detachments linked to bigger units by radio and tasked with reconnaissance or combat missions as far as fifty kilometres ahead of the cavalry divisions.

ARTILLERY AND SUPPLY UNITS

In the artillery, a clever employment of horse-drawn supply units had led to the creation of units unforeseen by the Treaty of Versailles.

Various services that has been formerly dispersed among regiments (signals, weather, topography, sound and light ranging) were gathered together into units. Thus, two observation groups equipped with fast vehicles were created. The seven regimental motorised batteries became once more anti-aircraft batteries, and the model 1914 self-propelled flak vehicles were transformed back for certain types of fire-power that were, however, forbidden.

Each regiment had at its disposal a partially motorised signals battery that comprised, amongst others, trucks and vans for telephone and radio, as well as motorcycles.

In liaison with supply units, experimental motorised units were created:

- two motorised batteries, one for light artillery, the other for heavy artillery
- a gas or artificial fog emitting battery (smoke) that was totally motorised with commercial type cars and trucks
- observation and spotting groups
- Flak batteries.

In term of materiel, a 10.5 cm field howitzer, a 7.7 cm howitzer and a 8.8 cm anti-aircraft gun were undergoing trials.

As with the other weapons, the artillery's prime concern was the improvement of unit manœuvrability skills (by generalising motorisation as much as possible) and making command organisation more flexible.

As for the mechanised supply units—seven detachments and twenty-four companies, three of which were anti-tank—they now were capable of undertaking combat missions. Pushing the policy of camouflaging materiel to its paroxysm, it had become the core and mobilising organ of all motorised units.

The government tried to make as many everyday vehicles as possible capable of being used by the army: liaison cars, four-wheel drive trucks and vans, agricultural tractors (tracked or wheeled), light reconnaissance cars etc. Special production runs led to artillery tractors still in the design process, and Daimler and Mercedes Benz armoured cars.

The successive transformations that it had undergone over the course of four years had removed the supply train from its usual role of troop transportation, supplies and materiel. In liaison with other the other arms, it had become capable of taking part in the battle too. And with its current organisation and composition, it constituted an extra element of strength and mobility.

ENGINEERS AND SIGNALS

In the engineers there were no notable changes made to the regulations in vigour, and there was no great bending of the clauses of the Treaty except for the issuing of flame-throwers (banned weaponry) to a divisional engineers battalion.

Concerning tactical matters, the command showed an increasing interest in the crossing of water obstacles:

- by day, for troops on foot, armoured cars, light artillery pieces, by using mobile equipment (rubber dinghies, powered boats or pontoon boats)

- at night, by the construction of bridges.

In the signals units, the mechanisation of divisional battalions was almost complete for radio and telephone companies. For the latter, all the horse drawn vehicles used by construction teams had not yet been replaced.

During the 1932 manoeuvres, each divisional staff had a motor vehicle and a code-making machine. There was also a six-group listening company.

However, the one-watt radio with a ten kilometre telephone range and a forty kilometre telegraph range, designed by the Telefunken company, was not quite yet in service.

MILITARY TRAINING-PREPARATION

13 September 1932 saw the creation, by decree, of the national bureau for youth education. This was the foreseen outcome of the joint efforts made by the German government and military command.

After having absorbed the organisation responsible for the military training of students, this new institution, the leadership of which was handed to General Otto von Stülpnagel, was tasked with training other ranks from organisations, junior officers recruited from the university elite and perfecting the training of officers and NCOs from an already trained reserve. There was no doubt that this was laying the foundations of an obligatory military service. It was the beginning of the end of a system imposed by the Treaty;

A battery of 7.7 cm (F.K. 16) field guns in position.

one could expect to see this program continued until its aims were achieved.

Furthermore, the voluntary work service, created by decree in July 1931, was met with such unanticipated success that the government incurred financial problems in order to retain the manpower, with numbers increasing from 300 in October 1931 to 275,000 at the end of 1932.

There were a million unemployed people aged between 18 and 26 and this constituted a considerable manpower pool, especially as here too, the admitted intentions concealed others. Although it is true that voluntary work was an act of national solidarity and the expression of both duty and discipline, the military character of the programs that were placed alongside the manual work left no doubt as to the real intentions. General Faulkner, who presided over the organisation asked for the work service to be made obligatory with a medical examination and lists of potential recruits.

AN APPRAISAL AT THE END OF 1933

By 1 April 1933, the total manpower was now over 100,000. Infantry battalions were now equipped with signals units and regiments had begun receiving infantry gun squads. Starting in this same month, during the annual training period, recruits were given an experimental complete basic training in the field. At Arys, Döberitz and Grafenwöhr, each battalion of these camps was increased to regiment size for a term thanks to the influx of SA men and other volunteers in order to render it operational. The training period was then concluded with manoeuvres undertaken alongside other *Reichswehr* regiments.

October saw the issuing of the latest version of the army field manual (*Truppenführung*).

Established in 1933, the peacetime program planned for:
• 21 infantry divisions within nine army corps
• a three-division cavalry corps
• motorised forces comprising of a light division by transforming the third cavalry division and a few mixed brigades by creating new units (reconnaissance, motorised infantry, motorised artillery...)
• general reserves.

The regiments and battalions were 'divided into three' and new units, signals, tanks, armoured cars, anti-tank and anti-aircraft

A sMG 08 heavy machine-gun is set up opposite the positions held by the 'enemy'.

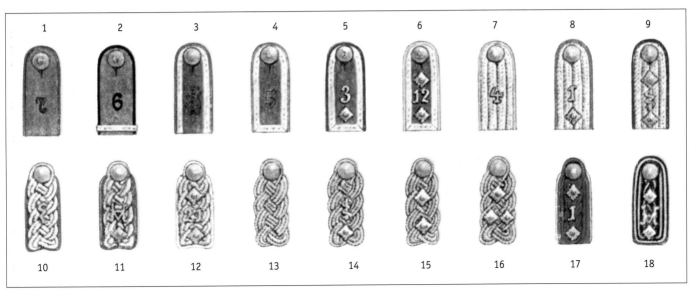

1. Private (light infantry)
2. NCO cadet (engineers)
3. NCO (artillery school)
4. NCO (signals)
5. Medical services sergeant
6. Sergeant (cavalry)
7. Second lieutenant (motorised supply train)
8. Lieutenant (mobile group)
9. Medical captain (medical services)
10. Veterinary major
11. Lieutenant-colonel (administration)
12. Colonel (infantry)
13. Brigadier general
14. General doctor inspector (medical services)
15. Army corps general
16. Army general
17. Bandmaster (infantry)
18. Chief cook

were progressively created. A certain number of staffs received the framework of the next staff echelon with the obvious aim of being used in the formation of new large units.

There was a plan to increase manpower to approximately 300,000 by 1 November 1934 and to 400,000 by the spring of 1935. In anticipation of obligatory national service, which would be reinstated in March 1935, the *Reichswehr* minister ordered the intensifying of pre-military training in order to avoid compromising quality for quantity. Thus, when inducted, the recruit would already be prepared and ready to join, the collective training of his unit without any transition.

The number of officers set by the Treaty of Versailles was 4,500, but the German army would need 20,000. In 1932, with some redundant officers kept on the books, there were some 5,000 officers, and at the end of 1933 this had increased to 8,000.

This number constantly increased thanks to measures taken by the High Command:

- a notable increase of members and the decrease in the length of lessons in officers' schools
- the nomination of NCOs as long as they were not promoted past the rank of captain

- the calling up of former second lieutenants and lieutenants as long as they were not promoted past the rank of captain. Although the publication of a new army field manual (*Truppenführung*) was announced, it would appear that the profound changes made to the organisation, composition and armament of the army did not change German theories, in fact it was quite the contrary.

With the war of movement designed to surprise the enemy whilst the latter was still preparing for war, there were two overriding factors to take into account:

1. The leader's rapidity of decision making, necessitating organisation that allows for intelligence gathering. Four or five reconnaissance and observation groups are being formed, the cavalry divisions have a divisional reconnaissance group and each army corps should have a reconnaissance group.

2. The rapidity of execution demanding sufficient possibilities to reduce potential resistance. This rests on the required mobility achieved by the development of motorised units and the decentralisation of artillery units, the divisional regiment being strengthened with a mixed heavy group of 15 cm howitzers and 10 cm guns.

CHANGES FROM 1934 TO 1935

By adopting the prudent rearmaments policies of his predecessors, Adolf Hitler continued the fulfilment of the *Umbau*. Initially defined by the 1932 plan, modified in the autumn of 1933 then in May 1934, the army was to reach a strength of 300,000 men by 1 May 1935 and to be able to field sixty-three divisions in the event of war. This final increase naturally posed a problem of reserves and led to, in liaison with the Nazi Party, the organisation of annual training for the 250,000 members of the Sturmabteilungen and the seven border guard battalions.

sons: two years prior to 1933, fourteen months for the 1933-35 intake. Further progress was made by the creation of three new schools in 1936, with Hanover, Munich and Potsdam joining Dresden.

2. In 1934-35, a certain number of NCOs (approximately 1,500) became officers, an increase in numbers that was necessary to ensure the training of recruits. Carefully selected, these NCOs perfectly prepared for their new roles and formed a precious source of junior officers.

3. In 1934, 3,500 retired, mothballed or reserve officers were integrated into the active army or placed on the supplemental officer roll (*Ergänzungsoffiziere*). In order to avoid any mediocrity, these

1. Automobile driver
2. Doctor in walking out dress with greatcoat
3. Quartermaster officer in service dress
4. Signals troop bandmaster

An armoured unit emblem at a parade in Berlin.

It was with this in mind that a new phase began, in 1934, of officer and NCO training, the building of new barracks, development of new weapons and the preparation of a new organisation for the autumn.

THE INCREASE IN STRENGTH

When the problem of its reorganisation appeared in 1933, the *Reichswehr* only had 4,300 officers. However, the program of thirty-six infantry divisions that it had set itself required approximately 30,000 officers. It is easy to see why the problem of officers was constantly at the top of the agenda.

There were four sources of recruitment available to solve the problem:

1. the increase in the number of officer cadets (180 in 1933, 300 in 1934, 1,000 in 1935) was made possible by a larger influx into the schools and a considerable decrease in the length of les-

officers underwent a rigorous selection process and took part in three or four month preliminary training courses.

4. In 1935, 2,000 officers of the Landespolizei were inducted into the army retaining their ranks, either on an individual basis or with their unit, with their morale value and professional qualities being their best guarantee.

The recruitment and training of reserve officers (*Offiziere des Beurlabtenstandes*), forbidden by the Treaty of Versailles, was officially re-established by the military laws of May 1935. Their corps was subdivided into reserve officers placed at the disposal of combatant units, and Landwehr officers for behind the lines service that could sent to combatant units, if need be.

The *Kriegsakademie* was created once again in Berlin to ensure the training of General Staff officers. Several technical schools were opened, such as the *Waffenmeisterschule* for masters at arms, the *Feuerwerkerschule* for artificers, and the *Nachrichtenschule* for signallers.

In all, there were approximately 13,000 in the active army. It is obvious that a great effort had been made in order to achieve this result, but the growth of large units and the increase in officers was probably far from being synchronised. It is possible that other forms of action would have to be set in motion in order for officer manpower to fulfil the already considerable and ever increasing needs of the new army.

The increasing number of large units that had begun in 1934 led to the application of measures designed to supply this new army with sufficient manpower. Short term service was authorised for a period of 18 months in the spring of 1934 and for one year in the autumn of the same year.

Thus, in that year, manpower increased from 120,000 to 300,000 men. This increase and that planned for 1936 required extra men. The problem was keenly felt within the artillery, engineers and signals, especially as the newly-formed *Luftwaffe* also needed manpower.

Of course, some manpower was provided by the first recruits that arrived in the barracks on 1 November 1935 and by the integration of the police units, of which 2,500 were officers, something that had been planned for a long time and which came into effect on 1 October 1935.

In order to increase the numbers of other ranks, soldiers were given the option, until 30 September 1935, to serve for a longer

Light Machine Gun MG08/15.

3

4

period of time. Preparation for this reorganisation began on 1 April and was generally split into several periods of time in order to keep it secret for as long as possible, the aim being to form ten army corps and twenty-three infantry divisions. Also, the reorganisation involved the creation of brand new units such as divisional reconnaissance groups, motorcycle rifle battalions, tank regiments, machine-gun battalions, signals battalions and so on.

Througout the course of 1935, the system of dividing units into three, as planned in 1932 in the event of conflict, the German High Command tripled the number of divisions that it was permitted to retain by the Treaty of Versailles. Also, it had begun the motorisation of large units by transforming a cavalry division into a motorised infantry division.

In the spring of 1935, a small number of specialists and future officers and NCOs were inducted as voluntary recruits. During the summer, the application of new military laws made it possible to carry out a census of men of the class of 34 (the first class for obligatory military service) who would be apt or exempt for military service. Out of the 549,000 registered, 450,000 (76%) were declared apt for service, and 35,000 (6%) apt under certain conditions. Then, in November, in order to increase the number of trained reservists and junior leaders for the arrival of the class of '35, the first of the 'birth deficit' classes, it recruited 90,000 volunteers from the classes of '30-'33 and 160,000 from the class of '34.

Thus, given the 40,000 men enlisted into the navy, air force or recruited into the police and SS, there remained approximately 250,000 men from the class of '34 that would be available to make up for the deficiencies of the following class.

At the beginning of March 1936, strength stood at approximately 480,000 men of whom there were:

- 90,000 professional former *Reichsheer* soldiers
- 90,000 soldiers recruited in 1934 and who extended their service in 1935
- 50,000 Lapo personnel incorporated into the army
- 160,000 men called up from the class of '34 who arrived in the barracks on 1 November 1935.

1935 was the year in which manpower was increased and new divisions created, but it also saw the creation of large peacetime

---

GRUPPENKOMMANDO I
Berlin—Eastern Borders
- 3. Panzer-Division (Berlin)

I. Armee-Korps
(Königsberg), near Polish borders
- 1. ID (Insterburg)
- 11. ID (Allenstein)
- 21. ID (Elbing)

II. Armee-Korps
Stettin, near Polish borders
- 2. ID (Stettin)
- 12. ID (Schwerin)

III. Armee-Korps
Berlin, near Polish borders
- 3. ID (FranKfurt am Oder)
- 13. ID (Magdeburg)
- 23. ID (Potsdam)

VIII. Armee-Korps
Breslau, Silesia, front of Poland and Czechoslovakia
- 8. ID (Oppeln)
- 18. ID (Liegnitz)

GRUPPENKOMMANDO II
Kassel—Western Borders
- 2. Panzer-Division (Wurzburg)

V. Armee-Korps
(Stuttgart), near the demilitarized zone
- 5. ID (Ulm)
- 15. ID (Wurzbourg)

VI. Armee-Korps
Munster, near the demilitarized zone
- 6. ID (Bielefeld)
- 16. ID (Munster)

IX. Armee-Korps
Kassel, near the demilitarized zone
- 9. ID (Giessen)
- 19. ID (Hanover)

GRUPPENKOMMANDO III
Dresden—Southern Borders
- 1. Panzer-Division (Weimar)

IV. Armee-Korps
Dresden, near Czechoslovakian Borders
- 4. ID (Dresden)
- 14. ID (Leipzig)
- 24. ID (Chemnitz)

VII. Armee-Korps
Munich, near Czechoslovakian and Austrian Borders
- 7. ID (Munich)
- 10. ID (Ratisbonne)
- 17. ID (Nuremberg)
- Gebirgsbrigade (Munich)
  - Gebirgs-Jäger-Regiment 98 (in 1937)
  - Gebirgs-Jäger-Regiment 99
  - Gebirgs-Jäger-Regiment 100
  - Gebirgs-Artillerie-Abteilung

X. Armee-Korps
Hamburg, North-Western Germany

- 20. ID (Hamburg)
- 22. ID (Bremen)

CAVALRY
- 1. KD (Potsdam)
  1. Brigade (Stettin)
  KR 5 (Stolp)
  KR 6 (Schwedt)
  2. Brigade (Hanover)
  KR 13 (Hanover)
  KR 14 (Ludwiglust)
  Aufklärungs-Abteilung (mot.) 8 (Potsdam)
- 2. KD (Breslau)
  3. Brigade (Breslau)
  KR 8 (Brieg)
  KR 10 (Rathenow)
  4. Brigade (Potsdam)
  KR 3 (Hanover)
  KR 9 (Fürstenwalde)
  Aufklärungs-Abteilung (mot.) 9 (Lüben)
- 5. *Reiterbrigade* (Insterburg)
  RR 1 (Insterburg)
  RR 2 (Angerburg)
  RR 4 (Allenstein)
  Radfahr Bataillon 1 (Tilsitt)
  leichte Artillerie Abteilung 5 (Insterburg)
  Kraftfahr-Abteilung Königsberg

KD	Kavalerie-Division
KR	Kavalerie-Regiment
RR	Reiter-Regiment

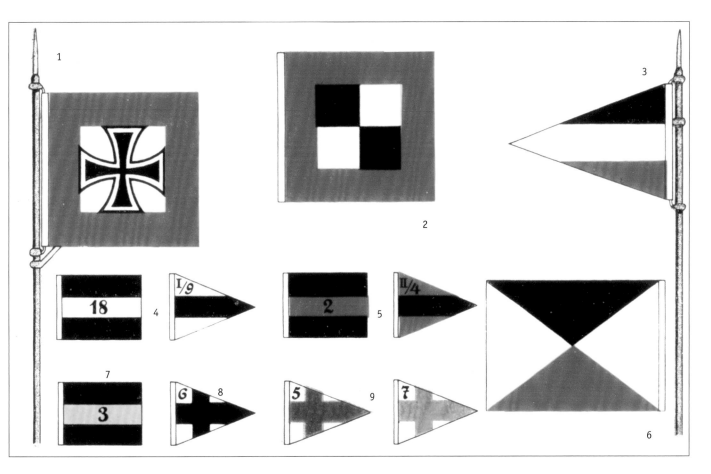

units along a "wartime" type organisation with organic units such as engineers, signals and medical services. In addition to the increase in manpower and the number of large units that it rendered possible, the November 1935 intake contained the beginnings of another development, as we will see when a certain number of all arms-of- service units allowed for the creation of new divisions in the Rhineland on 7 March 1936.

TRAINING AND MORALE

Since the begining of 1935, reservists aged 25 to 35 (classes that had never undertaken military service) received regular training. Generally volunteers, they were incorporated for two-month periods into special, but minor units, known as Ergänzungseinheiten, representing approximately sixty infantry battalions, twenty batteries, and as many engineer companies, plus twelve signals companies. This totalled approximately 200,000 reservists that received training in 1935.

It would appear that the personnel of these units were intended for the border units (Grenzschutz) positioned along the Polish and Czechoslovakian borders.

PENNANTS AND GUIDONS
1. *Heeresleitung* chief
2. *Gruppe* commander
3. Cavalry division
4. Infantry regiment and battalion
5. Artillery regiment and group
6. *Wehrkreis* commander
7. Cavalry regiment
8. Engineers battalion
9. Signals battalion headquarters (staff)

The execution of the main opposition in 1934 put an end to the rivalry between the army and some elements of the National-Socialist Party. Following this bloody episode that completed the victory of the military party, Hitler, in return, integrated the army into the National-Socialist state. It was by changing the old black, white and red flag for the swastika that this was most obvious.

However, although the army owed its renaissance to the new regime, the guiding spiritual force remained the indestructible apparatus of the former *Reichsheer*. This could be seen in the continuation of old traditions and the spirit of those who had received the indelible stamp of the old military regime.

Orchestrated by the propaganda of its leaders, the military renaissance signified for Germany its liberation from the Versailles 'Diktat' and the capacity to be master of its own destiny. The *Wehrmacht*, symbol of this re-found strength, was once more at the

A 10.5 cm LFH 18 light howitzer is put into position during an exercise.

Concealed name	Garrison	Normal name	*Wehrkreis*
— *Artillerieführer* I	Königsberg	1. ID	I
— *Artillerieführer* II	Stettin	2. ID	II
— *Kommandant von Frankfurt*	Frankfurt/Oder	3. ID	III
— *Artillerieführer* IV	Dresden	4. ID	IV
— *Kommandant von Ulm*	Ulm	5. ID	V
— *Artillerieführer* VI	Bielefeld	6. ID	VI
— *Artillerieführer* VII	Munich	7. ID	VII
— *Artillerieführer* III	Oppeln	8. ID	VIII
— *Infanterieführer* V	Giessen	9. ID	IX
— *Kommandant von Regensburg*	Ratisbonn	10. ID	XIII
— *Infanterieführer* I	Allenstein	11. ID	I
— *Infanterieführer* II	Schwerin	12. ID	II
— *Infanterieführer* IV	Magdeburg	13. ID	XI
— *Kommandant von Leipzig*	Leipzig	14. ID	IV
— *Artillerieführer* V	Wurzburg	15. ID	IX
— *Kommandant von Münster*	Münster	16. ID	VI
— *Infanterieführer* VII	Nuremberg	17. ID	XIII
— *Infanterieführer* III	Liegnitz	18. ID	VIII
Artillerieführer VI	Hanover	19. ID	XI
— *Reichswehrdienststelle Hamburg*	Hamburg	20. ID	X
— *Kommandant von Elbing*	Elbing	21. ID	I

forefront of the nation. The swearing of the oath of loyalty by all personnel was the realisation of an unconditional bond. The spirit of the officer class remained that of the former *Reichsheer*. Officers and NCOs came from the professional army or from rigorously selected recruits and were animated by a enthusiasm that was tinged with a certain fanaticism.

The re-establishment of military service in Germany seen as a real victory with militarised national socialism was the reason for the army's resurrection. Its leaders made sure that they called upon the other ranks' patriotism and sense of duty to the Führer, thus ensuring the continuation of traditions that had always fuelled the German army.

By the end of 1934 there were nine army corps, twenty-one infantry divisions, a mechanised infantry division and two cavalry divisions.

Then the following year, with the re-establishment of obligatory military service and the training of reservists, a new step was taken towards the goal set by the Führer: twelve army corps and thirty-six divisions.

ARMY CORPS

Nine army corps commands (*Korpskommandos*) were created in October 1934, the first seven coming from staffs of the infantry divisions allowed by the Treaty of Versailles:

- I army corps in Königsberg from the 1st Division.
- II army corps in Stettin from the 2nd Division.
- III army corps in Berlin from the 3rd Division.
- IV army corps in Dresden from the 4th Division.
- V army corps in Stuttgart from the 5th Division.
- VI army corps in Münster (Westphalia) from the 6th Division.
- VII army corps in Munich from the 7th Division.

Two were created from local Heeresdienststellen:

- VIII army corps in Breslau.
- IX army corps in Kassel.

Then, with the November 1935 incorporation in view, *Gruppenkommando* III was created, whilst the X army corps was created on 15 October in Hamburg from the cavalry corps command and elements of Wehrkreis II.

Each army corps comprised two or three infantry divisions as well as organic elements. They were not all complete However and the creation of some was not finished until October 1935, or even the mobilisation of 1939.

INFANTRY DIVISIONS

The formation of infantry divisions was rendered possible by the arrival of new men during the winter of 1934-35, with the existing units leading to the creation of new ones.

In order to conceal this increase, unit numbers disappeared and were replaced by the unit's garrison place name.

Then, on 15 October 1935, with the need to conceal units gone, the twenty-one 'concealed' formations were given the name of Infanterie-Division as well as a number:

Three divisions were formed directly thanks to the November 1935 intake: 22. ID in Bremen (WK X), 23. ID in Potsdam (WK III) and 24. ID in Chemnitz (WK IV).

Each comprised:

• three infantry regiments in theory comprising:

- three battalions of three rifleman or skirmisher companies (three platoons of three combat squads each armed with an automatic weapon) and one machine-gun company (three platoons and two semi-squads armed with two 20 mm guns)

- 13 mortar company

- 14 anti-tank company of three squads each armed with three 37 mm guns

• a three-group light artillery regiment (or field)

• a heavy artillery group with a horse drawn group and a motorised group (most of these had their own staff)

• a signals detachment

• an engineers battalion

Barrel transporters of a 15 cm gun battery parade in Nuremberg in November 1935.

• an anti-tank group

• an artillery observation group

• a medical detachment

In peacetime, the divisions contained the organic elements planned for wartime. Although the divisional reconnaissance group was not yet created, it was due to be during the course of 1936.

However, all of the divisions did not have the totality of their organic units and some units were only attached or created in the following years.

To this should be added a two-regiment mountain brigade Gebirgsbrigade of light mountain infantry, created in Garmisch-Partenkirchen (WK VIII).

CAVALRY DIVISIONS

It was initially planned to have one motorised cavalry division, named leichte Division (light division), formed by taking personnel from normal infantry divisions, with its motorised combat elements coming under the *Kraftfahrtruppen*. As for the two existing cavalry divisions, they would each receive a motorised reconnaissance group comprised an armoured car company, a cyclist company and a heavy company (anti-tank guns, pioneers).

However, the formation of the *leichte Division*, that was begun in 1934, was not completedsince it actually led to the creation, in October 1935, of one of the three armoured divisions now integrated into the special motorised troop arm.

ARMAMENT AND VEHICLES

At the end of 1936, the _Reichswehr_ had at its disposal materiel that had generally been brought into service during the Great War.

However, some more modern equipment began being issued. Nevertheless, it was obvious that the constraints and restrictions set by the Treaty of Versailles had considerably held up testing and manufacture which, at least initially, had to be carried out in secret.

ALL ARMS WEAPONS
● The **P08 pistol** or _Pistole 08 Luger_ had been the German army's regulation pistol since 1908. It fired 9 mm parabellum rounds contained in an eight-round box magazine and weighed 850 g without ammunition.
● The **98 pattern Mauser rifle** and 'carbine' (_Gewehr 98_ and _Karabiner 98K_) were the regulation weapons of the German army. They were 7.92 mm calibre and took 5-round clips. The Kar 98K measured 1 m 10 and weighed approximately 4 kg. The Gew 98 rifle had the same characteristics but with a

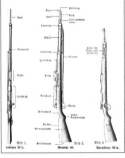

longer barrel and, consequently, a greater weight.
● The **24 pattern stick-gre-**

nade (_Stielhandgranate_ **24**) weighed 600 g and measured 35.6 cm in length. A metal transport case contained 15 grenades and 15 detonators. The 34 pattern (_Nebelhandgranate_ **34**) derived from this grenade.

Several types of machine-guns, firing the same ammunition as the Mauser rifle, were in service:
● **l.M.G. 08/15** in service during the Great War and used by the majority of infantry units. It weighed 15 kg and had a 300 round per minute rate of fire. Its optimal range was 800/2000 m and was water cooled. It had a bipod and could be used with a telescopic tripod for anti-aircraft fire. It could also be fired whilst moving.
● **l.M.G. 08/18** brought into service at the end of the war and equipping 'light infantry' units. Weighing 13 kg, its rate of fire was 500 rounds per minute. It had an optimal range of 800/2 000 m. The weapon was water cooled and fed with 250-round belts. It had a telescopic tripod for anti-aircraft fire.
● **l. M.G. 13** (Dreyse model) in service with the cavalry and motorised troops. It weighed 12 kg and could fire 300 rounds per minute with an optimal range of 800/2 000 m. The weapon was water-cooled and fed with 250-round belts.

Only one type of heavy machine-gun was in service:
● **s.M.G. 08** in service in the

Great War. With a 7.9 mm calibre, its rate of fire was 450/550 rounds per minute. Maximum range was 2,500 m. The gun was belt fed.

Weight with sledge mount, 64 kg, with tripod mount, 56 kg.

Anti-tank weapon
● As well as the anti-tank units within the cavalry regiments and reconnaissance groups, the sole anti-tank weapon in the arsenal, the _Panzerabwehrkanone_ **3,7 cm Pak**, was also in service in infantry units with:
— nine pieces in regimental motorised ant-tank companies
— twenty-seven pieces in divisional motorised anti-tank groups.

It weighed 400 kg and had a range of 550 metres. It fired armour piercing and explosive shells with a muzzle velocity of 760 m per second. Its rate of fire was 8 to 10 rounds per minute and it could pierce 33 mm of armour at a range of 600 m at a 60° incidence. The mount had an opening trail and the shells were carried in cases of twelve.

INFANTRY
Machine-guns (_Maschinengewehr_)
A new 7.92 mm calibre weapon was planned to soon equip the infantry units
● **M.G 34**
Weighing 12 kg with bipod (light version) and had an effective range of 1,800 m
The heavy version with tripod weighed 31 kg and had an effective range of 3,500 m. The weapon was air cooled and fed with 50-round belt with a maximum rate of fire of 800/900 rounds per minute with double 75-round drums. It could fire single shot or in bursts. A 50-round drum also existed.
● **Mortar (_Granatwerfer_)**
As was the case with the M.G. 34, it was planned to equip the infantry with a 8 mm mortar.
● **the _schwerer Granatwerfer_ 34 or s.Gr.W. 34.** Weighing 57

kg, it could be transported by three men or placed on a horse-drawn cart. Its effective range varied between 400 to 1,200 m. Its rate of fire was 6 rounds in 8 seconds, but the normal rate was 15 to 20 rounds per minute. The explosive shell weighed 3.5 kg.

Infantry support weapons (_Infanteriegeschütz_)
● Without doubt one of the most effective infantry support weapons, **the leichtes 7,5 cm _Infanteriegeschütz_** – also known as **_leichter Minenwerfer_ 18 or l.M.W. 18** in certain period texts, was intended for plunging or flat trajectory fire and could also be used, if need be, for defence against tanks. Crewed by six men, it was delivered in 1927 and six years later equipped the gun companies of infantry regiments, with six per infantry regiment and two per motorcycle battalion, motorised riflemen battalion, reconnaissance group and machine-gun squadron.
● Mounted on steel artillery wheels, the **leIG 18** was pulled by six horses or a tractor. Its weight in battery was 400 kg. For mule transport, it could be broken down into six loads of 75 kg maximum. It had a range of 3,500 m and a maximum rate of fire of 15 to 20 rounds per minute. Muzzle velocity was 225 m per second and the explosive shell weighed 5.5 kg.
● A heavy model, **the _schweres Infanteriegeschütz_ 15 cm sIG 33**, was planned to be put into service within the same units. Crewed by nine men, it weighed 1,500 kg. It was horse-drawn or towed by a vehicle. With a range of 5,500 m, it fired explosive and smoke shells at a rate of 15 to 20 rounds per minute.

CAVALRY AND ARMOUR
Made by Daimler-Benz from 1932 to 1934, the light machine-gun carrying armoured car – _Maschinengewehrkraftwagen_ or _Panzerspähwagen_ – was developed between 1929-32 for reconnaissance missions and delivered to motorised units in the process of being formed. Grouped in eight-vehicle troops, it was entered into the composition of mixed armoured car companies.

Weight: 2,100 kg, crew: 2 men serving a MG 13 with 1,000 rounds
Maximum speed: 60 km/h, range: 240 km

A model designed around the same chassis – **Funkkraftwagen** – was equipped with a long-range radio. It had a crew of three and was not armed with a machine-gun.

Other vehicles were on the verge of being delivered to formations:
● a heavy six-wheeled armoured vehicle (_Strassenpanzerwagen_ which became **the schwere _Panzerspähwagen_ 6-Rad**), the construction of which was ordered in 1929 and which was due to equip mixed reconnaissance group companies from 1936 onwards, weight: 6 t, crew: 4 men armed with a 20 mm machine-gun, maximum speed: 60 km/h, armed with a MG 13.

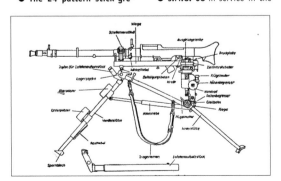

● A light tank initially known as **the Zweimanntank** then **Panzerkampfwagen I** designed in 1933 under the concealed name of Landwirtschaftlicher Schlepper (agricultural tractor).

From 1934, when concealment was no longer necessary, several models of tank were put into production:

● *Panzerkampfwagen* I **Ausf. A**

Weight: 3.5 t, two-man crew without turret. The fifteen tanks made between February and April were used for training the crews of the two armoured regiments of *Kraftfahrlehrkommando* at Zossen and Ohrdruf.

Weight: 5.4 t, with a two-man crew armed with two turret-mounted MG 13.

Construction began in July 1934 and the first tanks were delivered in September and July 1935 with *Kraftfahrlehrkommando* receiving 475.

● *Panzerkampfwagen* I **Ausf. B**

Weight: 5.8 t, two-man crew armed with two turret-mounted MG 13.

Construction began in August 1935 and the first tanks were delivered to all armoured units. They differed from the

previous type by a more powerful engine.

Weight 4 t, two-man crew without turret. Also known as **Instandsetzungskraftwagen I**, it equipped breakdown and maintenance units of tank companies.

● *kleine Panzerbefehl swagen*

Weight: 5.9 t with a three-man crew armed with a single MG 13. This was a command tank first built in 1935 and which equipped all the tank formations, from company to brigade level.

The mixed armoured car company comprised of:

— A command troop comprising, in particular, two unarmed armoured cars equipped with radio transmitters

— a heavy troop with six heavy machine-guns

— a combat and supply column.

The light tank troop comprised of:

— an car (Kübelsitzwagen)

— a tank for the troop commander

— two groups each with three tanks

— a triple-axle all-terrain vehicle **(Mannschaftwagen)** transporting the troop commander replacement and twelve replacement men.

The artillery used a certain number of guns and howitzers of various calibres, either types that had been used in the Great War or those designed between 1926 and 1930 (indicated by the number 18). There was no heavy artillery in the general reserve as this had been forbidden by the Treaty of Versailles.

● **7.7 cm** *Feld Kanone* **16**

Weight when transported: 2,250 kg, range: 10,700 m, elevation: 40°

Weight in battery: 1,400 kg, traverse: 4°

This field gun was used during the Great War and was partially replaced in 1934 by a new model known as the 7.5 cm FK 16 n/A (neuer Art), achieved by placing a 7.5 cm barrel on the old mounting, increasing the range to approximately 12,000 m.

● **7.5 cm** *Gebirgskanone* **15**

Weight in battery: 630 kg, range: 3 900-6 600 m, elevation: - 9° to + 50°, transported by mule in seven loads, the heaviest of which, the removable shield, weighed 156 kg. Traverse: 7°.

The 7.5 cm GebK 15 was purchased from the Czech Skoda factories in the first years of the *Reichswehr*. It equipped the group, then the artillery brigade of the mountain brigade stationed in Bavaria.

● **leichte 10,5 cm** *Feldhaubitze* **16**

Weight in battery: 1,450 kg, range: 3,400-9,200 m, elevation: - 4° to + 40°

weight for transportation: 3,300 kg, traverse: 4°.

The light field howitzer then became the only light divisional gun.

The 10.5 cm le FH 16 was in service with the light horse-drawn groups and automobile groups. For the latter, the gun was transported on a set of wheels or a four-wheel trailer.

● **leichte 10.5 cm** *Feldhaubitze* **18** *für Kraftzug*

Weight in battery: 1,985 kg, weight: 3,600-10,400 m, ele-

vation: - 6° to + 40°, weight for transportation: 3,300 kg, traverse: 56°.

This new twin-trail gun was designed with automobile towing in mind. The 10.5 cm le FH 18 began replacing the 16 model within motorised units in 1936. Also intended to be horse-drawn in two loads in the same groups of the 15 cm sFH 18 heavy howitzer.

● **10 cm** *Kanone* **17**

Weight in battery: 3,300 kg, maximum range: 14,000 m, elevation: 6°, traverse: 45°. It could be broken down into two loads for road transport: barrel vehicle 3,000 kg and mounting vehicle 3,300 kg. A Great War gun, the 10.5 cm le K 17 still equipped some batteries of the heavy-horse-drawn groups within divisions.

● **schwere 10 cm** *Kanone* **18**

Weight in battery: 5,640 kg, range: 13,000/18,000 m, elevation: 0° to 48°

Projectile weight: 16 kg, elevation: 64°.

Developed from 1926-30, the s 10 cm K 18 was brought into service in 1933-34 within some divisional horse-drawn heavy battery groups.

● *schwere* **15 cm** *Feldhaubitze* **13.**

Weight in battery: 5,640 kg, effective range: 8,300 m, elevation: 4°

Road transportation weight: 3,000 kg, elevation: 45°.

Issued to units in 1917, the s 15 cm FH 13 was still in use within some divisional horse-drawn heavy group batteries. It was usually towed by a team of six horses.

● *schwere* **15 cm** *Feldhaubitze* **18** *für Kraftzug*

Weight in battery: 5,500 kg, range: 4,000-13,000 m, elevation: - 3° to + 45°, weight of projectile: 40 kg, traverse: 64°

This was a new split trail gun made with automobile towing in mind. The 15 cm sFH 18 equipped motorised divisional batteries. It could also be transported by horses and broken down into two loads.

● **15 cm** *Kanone* **16**

Weight in battery: 11,000 kg, effective range: 22,000 m, elevation: 6°, traverse: 43°.

Brought into service in 1917, the 15 cm K 16 continued to equip some batteries of divisional horse-drawn heavy groups.

● **15 cm** *Kanone* **18**

Weight in battery: 10,000 kg, effective range: 22,000 m, elevation: 8°, transported in two loads, traverse: 45°.

(All photographs are "Private Collection, All Rights Reserved)

The 15 cm K 18 was intended to equip some motorised divisional heavy groups.

● *lange* **21 cm** *Mörser*

Weight in battery: 6,700 kg, effective range: 11,000 m, elevation: 4°. Weight for road transportation: 12,000 kg, traverse: 45°, transported in three loads: barrel 4,200 kg, mounting 4,500 kg, chassis 3,300 kg.

The Lg 21 cm Mrs was brought into service in 1916. It was to be replaced by it with an equivalent, more up to date gun within divisional artillery of the general reserve.

ANTI-AIRCRAFT DEFENCE

● **2 cm** *Flugabwehrkanone* **30**

Weight in battery: 483 kg, vertical range: 100 to 1,645 m, horizontal range: 1,600 m, elevation: - 12° to + 90° Rate of fire: 280 rounds per minute, traverse: 60° on a platform. Rate of fire on a trailer: 120 rounds per minute.

Manufactured at the end of the 1920s, the 2 cm Flak 30 was delivered to the navy in 1934 and entered into service with the Luftwaffe in 1935. Initially named the 2 cm Flak MG 30, it was used in the army to provide aerial defence against low-flying aircraft alongside three platoons each armed with four-machine guns (six men per MG).

● **3.7 cm** *Flugabwehrka-none* **18**

Weight in battery 1,750 kg, effective range 2,000 m, rate of fire: 160 rounds per minute, elevation - 8° to + 85°, effective rate of fire: 800 rounds per minute with 360° traverse on platform.

Brought into service in 1935, the 3.7 cm Flak 18 was the next size up from the 2 cm.

● **8.8 cm** *Flugabwehrka-none* **18**

Weight in battery: 6,500 kg, maximum vertical range: 10,000 m, transport weight: 7,000 kg, effective vertical range: 8,000 m, rate of fire 15-20 rounds per minute, horizontal range: 15,000 m, muzzle velocity: 820 m per second.

Ordered in 1925 by the Heeresleitung that deemed the 7.5 cm underpowered, the 8.8 cm Flak 18 or 'Acht-Acht' was brought into service in 1933. It was also used in heavy groups of Luftwaffe regiments in four-gun batteries alongside the Kommandogerät telemeter.

ENGINEERS

The German army was equipped with several types of pneumatic dinghies (Schlauchboote):

● small model for three to four men

● large model for twelve men with campaign equipment; it could also be used for a light 2 t 5 pontoon bridge or with a platform to allow for the transport cars or artillery pieces.

● **Materiel for the old type bridge** was still in service. This comprised two corrugated metal boats each weighing approximately 330 kg.

A single boat could carry the six-man crew (rudder man, four rowers, replacement rower) as well as:

— 18 men with light machine-guns,

— or two heavy machine-guns with their crews,

— or one light machine-gun with its crew and an ammunition cart.

The raft with two boats could carry the crew (an NCO, two rudder men, eight rowers) as well as:

— 60 men with light machine-guns,

— or six cavalrymen with their horses,

— or a machine-gun vehicle with trailer and men,

— or a field gun and front wheels, with three horses and men,

— or a gun, caisson and twelve men,

— or a 3 t 3 vehicle and horses on the platform.

The two-boat strengthened raft could transport, not including the crew:

— a vehicle not exceeding 5 tonnes,

— one to three 3 t 5 unloaded trucks,

— or a light machine-gun with its crew and ammunition cart.

The raft strengthened by three boats could transport, not including the crew:

— an automobile tractor with personnel,

— or a loaded 3 to 5 tonne truck.

Bridge construction was carried out by positioning and anchoring boats or rafts. One can identify a bridge built with 6, 4 or 3 edges according to the number of beams placed on 6, 4 or 3 edges.

The pontoon bridge equipment allowed for the construction of the following bridges:

● **footbridge** (four edge sections) built by two companies in two hours, length 150 m, for infantry in columns of two, cavalry one by one and artillery with gun crews on foot

● **light pontoon bridge** (4 edge sections) built by three engineer companies in two hours, length 120 m, for all units and vehicles weighing less than 3 t 5

● **strengthened pontoon bridge** (4 edge sections with strengthened span sections) built by three engineer companies in two and a half hours, length 120 m, for vehicles up to 5 tonnes

● **heavy platoon bridge** (6 edge sections) built by three to four engineer companies in two and a half hours, length 70 m, for vehicles up to 11 tonnes

and a 0.60 m gauge railway.

There was a new type of boat with the same characteristics as the previous model, but wider and heavier (720 kg instead of 330). A single boat could transport, not including the crew:

— a combat group,

— or two machine-guns, two ammunition carts and ten men,

— or a light mortar with its crew, equipped with an ammunition cart,

— or men and materiel.

● **A pontoon bridge** with cutwaters could double the vehicle tonnage capacity.

A new pattern pontoon bridge entered into service in 1935.

Transported on truck towed trailers (notably by trucks of the 3rd company of engineer battalions), it notably comprised sixteen metal boats on four-wheel trailers and two 100 hp powered dinghies with two wheels.

This allowed for the construction of a 110 m bridge with a 6 tonne capacity, or 83 metres for 8 tonnes, or 30 metres for 10 tonnes with trestles only.

In the cavalry, there now only existed two divisions and an independent brigade formed around existing elements.

Each division comprised:

• Two cavalry brigades each with two regiments including a staff, a motorised squadron, four horse squadrons and a machine-gun squadron.

• a horse-drawn artillery group

• a motorised engineers group

• a signals group

• a motorised reconnaissance group

- staff and signals section

- an armoured car company and a motorcyclist company

- a heavy company (command platoon, towed light mortar platoon, three-gun towed anti-tank platoon, pioneer platoon).

General reserves

Nine battalions of motorised machine-gunners were formed at the end of October 1935 with five based along the demilitarised zone and four on the southern and eastern borders, seemingly as covering units. Each had a staff, signals platoon, three combined machine-gun companies and a motorcycle unit with one or several platoons.

There also existed:

— the Bamberg cavalry group formed from the 15th, 17th and 18th regiments disbanded in the spring of 1936, the organic reconnaissance groups of the infantry divisions

— three anti-tank defence detachments, stationed near the demilitarised zone

— four motorised reconnaissance groups, intended to be part of the future formation of army corps reconnaissance groups.

CHANGES FROM 1934 TO 1935 (continued)
Infantry

October 1935 saw the creation of regimental support units:

— signals platoon (*Nachrichtenzug*) and horse platoon (*Reiterzug*)

3.7 cm (Pak 36) gun and its tractor changing its firing position.

A cavalry regiment crossing a river obstacle,
the men are using a 'S' rubber dinghy.

An old model metal boat that could transport a strong combat group,
notably equipped with light machine-guns

— support company (*Schützenkompanie*) with nine light machine-guns, 2 heavy machine-guns and three light mortars

— machine-gun company (*MG Kompanie*) with a 4-heavy machine-gun platoon and a platoon of three groups each with two heavy mortars

— infantry gun company (*Infanterie-Geschütz-Kompanie*) equipped with 6 light guns and two heavy guns

— motorised anti-tank company (*Panzerabwehrkompanie*) with four platoons each with three guns

— support group (*leichte Infanteriekolonne*) to be formed upon mobilisation.

The 4th battalion that still had a few regiments could form the core of new regiments that were due to be formed.

On 1 March 1936, there were 77 regiments: sixty-nine numbered from 1 to 69, three bearing numbers 75, 84 and 87, three from Saxony and Thuringia (101, 102, 103) and two mountain regiments (99 and 100).

Cavalry

In 1935, the development of the cavalry was carried out according to the accelerated rate of motorisation. This transformation had two objectives: the almost entire disbanding of large cavalry units and the creation of a new arm, the armoured units.

But above all, a large scale transformation was planned for 1 April 1936. This transformation announced the deletion of cavalry divisions in the spring and affected large units and regiments. However, contrary to other arms of service, its strength was not increased.

Horse-drawn artillery groups were either motorised, or incorporated as they were into divisional artillery regiments.

The number of regiments was to be increased to twenty, with

seven brigade commands at Stettin, Breslau, Brieg, Dresden, Hanover and Insterburg.

The regimental heavy squadron was split up in order to create:

— a three-troop heavy machine-gun squadron (two vehicle borne and one mule transported) and a light mortar troop

— a motorised squadron comprising a command troop with three towed 3.7 cm guns and a pioneer troop.

Mechanised and motorised troops

The Treaty of Versailles forbade all armoured vehicles. This inferiority was even more keenly felt by the German general staff as they had assessed the tank's formidable effectiveness on the battlefield. Nonetheless, the *Reichswehr* high command did not place much faith in tanks. Plan 'A', that secretly prepared for the army's increase from seven to twenty-one divisions, only planned for one lone group of fifty-five light tanks.

Until 1933, the automobile element could only be found in the supply column units in the shape of seven groups forming an experimental and training element for motorisation and the motorisation of anti-tank defence. Although the bulk of transport was frequently carried out by automobile units during manoeuvres, the latter always included the use of enemy and friendly tanks, and a good anti-tank defence was constantly organised.

The groups that had retained the sole role and structure of a transport unit were progressively strengthened by specialist companies of motorcyclists, armoured cars and anti-tank guns. At the beginning of 1933, all the groups were transformed into combat units known as *Kraftfahrabteilungen*.

The men of these units were open-minded and understanding. To begin with, the seven groups of automobile supply, tasked with divisional transport and which, in peacetime, were hardly ever used, worked towards organising themselves as motorised combat formations. In this way, *Kraftfahr-Abteilung* 6 of Hanover can be considered the ancestor of the tank arm. 'Tank' training had been undertaken within its 2nd company since 1924, using fake tanks, whereas the 1st and 3rd companies were organised into motorcyclist riflemen. With the 3rd group in Berlin, the 1st company was equipped with reconnaissance armoured cars, the 2nd with tanks and the 3rd with anti-tank guns.

The rebuilding effort that after Hitler's coming to power was, therefore, directed particularly at the constitution of an autonomous tank arm.

On 1 July 1934, the automobile unit inspection at the ministry of defence, was split in two: *Inspektion für Heeresmotorisierung* for motorisation and *Inspektion der Kraftfahrkampftruppen*

A pontoon bridge built using old and new model boats.

or concealed command for combat tanks. At the head of these inspectorates was *Generalmajor* Oswald Lutz bearing the title of '*Kommandierender General der Panzertruppen, zugleich Inspekteur der Kraftfahrkampftruppen und der Heeresmotorisierung*'.

Under this high command, four motorised unit commands were created (*Kraftfahrkommandos*) in Berlin, Kassel, Munich and Königsburg.

Motorised reconnaissance groups were formed in the three cavalry divisions and each horse cavalry regiment had a motorised squadron known as *Stabsschwadron*, grouping together a command troop, towed anti-tank gun troop and pioneer troop.

As for the supply and transport units, 1934 saw it undergo the creation of motorised combat units known as *Kraftfahrkampftruppen* comprising armoured car, tank and motorcycle companies, as well as anti-tank groups (*Panzer-Abwehr Abteilungen*). The automobile units were split into three which allowed them to carry

The Enigma cipher machine.

out large scale troop movement exercises during the course of the summer of 1934.

The speed that the command sought and obtained by motorisation and mechanisation was the main quality of armoured and motorised troops.

The transformation of a cavalry division into a motorised infantry division in Weimar paved the way for the creation of large motorised units. In October 1935, three armoured divisions were created in part with motorised cavalry regiments (4th, 7th, 11th, 12th and 16th). This massive entrance onto the military stage showed how much importance the High Command placed on motorisation.

Endowed with a large offensive capability that was combined with, as much as possible, speed and mobility, this was a new special arm that was the fruit of the development of motorisation and the conditions of modern warfare.

Next to appear, in November 1935, were the first divisions:

• 1. Panzer-Division in Weimar (WK IX) from the light division, former-3rd cavalry division

• 2. Panzerdivision in Würzburg (WK XIII) and 3. *Panzerdivi-*

sion in Berlin (WK III), the creation of which was made possible by the November 1935 intake.

Each division comprised:
• divisional staff (headquarters)
• two-regiment armoured tank regiment
• reconnaissance brigade (or light)
- signals section
• two-battalion rifleman regiments each comprising:
- staff
- motorcyclist company
- two companies transported by all-terrain vehicles
- three-platoon machine-gun companies each comprising two semi-platoons with two guns (total of 12 guns)
- heavy company

INFANTRY
1. Sergeant-major in service dress
2. Private in walking-out uniform
3. Private with greatcoat
4. Drummer

1

2

- five-company motorcyclist battalion.
- Motorised reconnaissance group
  - staff (headquarters)
  - signals section
  - two motorcycle companies (one in peacetime)
  - heavy company
- anti-tank detachment
- motorised artillery group
- engineer units (unidentified)
- signals detachment (staff, motorised signals and radio companies)

Motorised or mechanised troops thus comprised:
— the armoured divisions, large mechanised units
— motorised reconnaissance groups of the armoured or cavalry divisions
— anti-tank groups or detachments.

Contrary to what is commonly believed, the armoured divisions did not immediately dispose of all their organic elements. They

3

4

were, nevertheless, sufficiently organised to train the personnel, carry out testing, and make their staff elements function correctly.

Artillery

During the course of 1935, the German command's efforts were aimed at achieving a twin objective:
— to equip new large units with the necessary artillery:
— increase the firepower of this artillery by developing heavy artillery and the adoption of powerful modern materiel.

In addition to the light and heavy artillery groups, it was planned to equip divisional artillery with observation groups.

At the divisional level, the materiel in service was as follows:
— the 7.5 cm field gun that entered into the composition in 1936 and was to be phased out for the 10.5 cm howitzer
— the 10.5 cm light howitzer that equipped light groups in 1934 with two batteries for one with 7.5 cm guns that it was in the process of replacing in order to become the sole light gun within the division.

At army corps level and in the general reserves, there were two split-tail heavy guns, towed in a single 6-tonne load in the motorised version, and two loads for the horse-drawn version: the 10 cm heavy gun and the 15 cm heavy howitzer.

Engineers

1935 saw the generalisation of motorisation that, up to that point, had been applied to a few formations. The goal of the increasing mobility and firepower was about to be achieved. The

With fixed bayonet, an infantryman charges towards the 'enemy'.

Artillerymen take place in a half-track tractor used both as a gun crew transport and ammunition carrier.

entry into service of new materiel now meant that the numerous engineer units were capable of rapidly carrying out their tasks.

The engineers, whose strength was due to eventually reach 32,000 men including schools, training centres and technical establishments, were to be capable of taking part in:

— fighting for water obstacles

— the organisation of strategic and tactical blocks

— the manoeuvring of large mechanised units.

Infantry combat training was dispensed up to and including company level. Engineer troops were under the command of the Heeresleitung, named *Inspektion der Pioniere* or In/5. This was an arm of service command. With each Gruppenkommando was a general officer (*Pionier Inspizient*) tasked with inspecting engineer units within the *Gruppenkommando*.

With each army corps was:

- an army corps engineers unit commander (colonel or lieutenant-colonel) aided by a staff section

- an army corps engineers battalion.

To each infantry division was attached an engineers battalion comprising:

• a motorised battalion headquarters.

• a motorised signals platoon.

• Two partially motorised companies with three platoons with three squads armed with a light machine-gun and equipped with two horse-drawn technical vehicles and a (*Munitions und Maschinen Trupp*) platoon equipped with three six-wheeled all-terrain trucks.

• a motorised company of identical composition to that of the partially motorised company, although the commander and the command group were equipped with automobiles and motorbikes.

• a motorised bridging team comprising:
- sixteen four-wheeled trailers with metal boats (800 kg approximately)
- two two-wheeled trailers with 100 hp powered dinghies.
- two all-terrain trucks carrying bridging equipment (trestles, beams, cross beams etc.)
• a motorised engineers materiel unit (*Pionier Gerät Staffel*) equipped with three all-terrain trucks transporting electric and pneumatic tools, pile drivers, compressors, electric generators etc.
• a light motorised engineers materiel column (equipment reserve).

The army corps engineers battalion was identical to the divisional engineers battalion with the only difference being its increased motorisation and the addition of a military band.

Signals

The actively pursued motorisation of 1935 brought into service all-terrain vehicles (trucks, vans, *Kübelsitz* cars) intended for the laying of telephone lines and also for use as radio vehicles, telephone exchanges and encryption workshops.

Research concerning the use of ultra-short waves was continued. The strength of signals units was due to reach a final figure of 24,000 men, including schools, training centres and technical establishments.

Signals personnel came under the command of the Heeresleitung named Inspektion der Nachrichten Truppen.

With each *Gruppenkommando* commander was a general officer (*Nachrichten Inzipient*) tasked with the inspection of signalling in the *Gruppenkommando*. Within each army corps, a colonel or lieutenant-colonel commanded the signals units stationed on the army corps' territory.

In wartime, organisation would be centralised into a single organ of the command of national defence signals, controlling the signals of the army, air force, navy, various ministerial departments and the propaganda services.

A new standard is presented to an artillery unit.

DIE KRIEGSMARINE

Reduced in size like the *Reichsheer* by the clauses of the Treaty of Versailles, the strength of the *Reichsmarine* was limited to 15,000 men, including 1,500 officers, a number that was insufficient to provide crews for the ships allowed by the Treaty: six old *Schlesien* cruisers that were already obsolete in 1914, six 6,000-tonne cruisers, twelve 800-tonne destroyers and twelve 600-tonne torpedo boats.

Submarines and an air arm were strictly forbidden and naval ship building was limited to 10,000-tonne ships.

The German navy was no more than *'a caricature of a 100,000-tonne war fleet* (144,000 including the reserve ships)' which was in all ways inferior to the other European fleets, except perhaps for operations in the Baltic.

In fact, the admirals did not agree on the war objective. Was it the destruction of enemy forces by a high seas fleet based around battleships as *Admiral Tirpitz* had sought, the control of lines of communication with a balanced fleet combining large ships with ships capable of a war of pursuit.

This last option, recommended by Rear-Admiral Wolfgang Wegener, demanded the rapid occupation of Norwegian ports and the capture of the French coast as far as Brest in order to control the Calais straits and access to the North Sea. This was turned down in 1926 as it was deemed ill-timed; the admiral left the navy.

THE GERMAN NAVY FROM 1921 TO 1934

The naval command tried all ways to increase the size of its fleet, in quantity and quality. The Washington disarmament conference and the negotiations could have given it a chance to do this, but the defence and foreign affairs ministers did not pay them any attention. Another solution was to begin modernising the fleet within the clauses of the Treaty, but with the objective of reaching an even footing with the French fleet.

This led to the laying down of five light cruisers and twelve 800-tonne destroyers between 1921 and 1928.

Then, as part of the *Umbau*, the *Reichsmarine* drew up a program intended for approaching an even footing with France and planning for a 'balanced strength' according to the recommendations of Admiral Erich Raeder, Commander-in-Chief of the navy since 1928. The program comprised of the laying down of six or eight battleships, three aircraft-carriers, seven heavy cruisers, twelve light cruisers, 82 destroyers and 80 torpedo boats. In fact, the initial construction was limited to four 2,200- tonne destroyers that were scheduled to enter into service in 1934.

At the same time, it was decided in 1928 to build a ship intended to replace one of the old *Schliesen* class ships. The *Panzerschiff Deutschland* totally adhered to the stipulations of the Treaty. With a displacement of 12,000 tonnes, it was armed with eight 280 mm guns and could reach a speed of 28 knots. Its range of 10 to 18,000 nautical miles, depending on its speed, was high and its guns outclassed all

The pocket battleship *Deutschland*.

of the heavy cruisers of the time that were only armed with 203 mm guns. Also, most of the other cruisers could only reach 22 knots at best. Laid down in February 1929, it entered into service in April 1933, followed in November 1934 by its sister ship the *Admiral Scheer,* then a little later by the *Admiral Graf Spee*. Immediately known as a 'pocket cruiser', the *Deutschland* caused concern in other navies and began a new naval arms race in 1930, notably in the French and Italian navies who quickly replied by laying down two 35,000-tonne ships each.

When Hitler came to power, he showed his opposition to Admiral Tirpitz's plans and seemed favourable, therefore, to the idea of a 'balanced strength' defended by Commander Karl Dönitz. Nevertheless, he remained prudent and circumspect and the sailors feared that his strategy was essentially land based

1. Admiral in parade uniform
2. Captain
3. Ensign
4. Senior bridge officer

and that the navy would thus be affected by this. It was only at the end of 1934 that Hitler authorised the laying down of two battleships and the first submarine in a series of twenty to be built as part of the 1935-36 program.

Hitler, in fact, increased pacifist declarations and wanted to retain at all costs the benevolent neutrality of Great Britain. If there was to be a 'balanced navy', it was only in the perspective of conflict with France and Poland. On the other hand, an alliance with Great Britain suited him, an alliance based on a sort of hegemonic sharing: the British with their empire and control of the seas and the German domination of continental Europe and expansion towards the east.

It was with this in mind that he signed the London naval agreement of 18 June 1935.

He obtained, however, a 450,000 tonne navy, but the sailors were disappointed as they still hoped to achieve equal footing with France. Be that as it may, new naval ship building was planned on top of the two battle cruisers already due to be laid down: two battleships, five heavy cruisers, two aircraft-carriers, destroyers, and ocean going and coastal defence submarines. These orders would keep naval shipyards busy until 1941.

The Anglo-German naval agreement of June 1935 was a sort of official birth certificate for the *Reich*'s new navy. This agreement freed Germany from the constraints of the Treaty of Versailles and set the development of its naval forces: 35% of the aggregate tonnage of the British Commonwealth of Nations and, concerning submarines, 45% and even 100% of the total tonnage of the British Commonwealth of Nations. In a nutshell, Great Britain was allowed to have approximately 1,200,000 tonnes, whereas Germany was authorised 420,000 tonnes.

THE TURNING POINT OF 1935

On 29 June 1935, Germany issued a communiqué concerning its new naval shipbuilding program:

— Two 26,000-tonne cruisers armed with nine 280 mm guns

NAVAL SHIP BUILDING

NAVAL SHIPYARDS

Bremen	*Deschimag*
Elbing	*Schichau*
Hambourg	*Blohm und Voss*
Kiel	*Krupp*
	Germania-Werft
	Deutsche Werke
Vegesack	*Lürssen*
Wilhelmshaven	*Reichsmarinewerft*
	then Kriegsmarinewerft

RESERVE SHIPS – CADET SCHOOLS *LINIEN-SCHIFFE*

● *Schlesien*

1904 budget laid down at Wilhelmshaven in 1905, launched 28.5.06, in service 1.3.27.

● *Schleswig-Holstein*

1904 budget laid down at Wilhelmshaven 1905, launched 17.12.06, in service 1.2.26.

CHARACTERISTICS
- tonnage: 6-7, 000 t.
- main armament: 4 x 28 cm + 6 x 10.5 cm Flak.
- speed: 16 knots range: 6,000 nautical miles at 10 nm/h.
- crew: 725 men.
Rebuilt in 1936, these ships were attached as school ships to training inspection (*Bildungs-Inspektion*) at Kiel.

● *Emden*

1921 budget laid down at Wilhelmshaven, 12.21, launched 7.1.25 in service 15.10.25.

CHARACTERISTICS
- tonnage: 6-7,000 t
- main armament: 8 x 15 cm + 8 x 8.8 cm Flak.
- speed: 29 knots range: 5,000 nautical miles 18 nm/h.
- crew: 630 men.
The first ship built for the Kriegsmarine after the Great War, this light cruiser was built according to plans designed in 1918.
It undertook many training sailings abroad as part of the Bildungs-Inspektion.

"POCKET BATTLESHIPS" *PANZERSCHIFFE*

● *Deutschland*

1928 budget laid down at Kiel in 1929, launched 19.5.31, in service 1.4.33.

● *Admiral Scheer*

1931 budget laid down at Wilhelmshaven in 6.31 launched 1.4.33., in service 12.11.34

● *Admiral Graf Spee*

1932 budget laid down at Wilhelmshaven in 1932 launched 30.6.34, in service 6.1.36.

CHARACTERISTICS
- tonnage: 12-16, 000 t-
- main armament: 6 x 28 cm- + 8 x 15 cm + 6 x 10.5 cm Flak
- speed: 28 knots-
- range: 22,000 nautical miles at 19 nm/h.
- crew: 1,150 men.

BATTLESHIPS *SCHLACHTSCHIFFE*

● *Scharnhorst*

1933 budget laid down at Wilhelmshaven in 1934, launched 3.10.36, in service 7.1.39.

● *Gneisenau*

1934 budget laid down at Kiel in 2.34, launched 8.12.36, in service 21.5.38.

CHARACTERISTICS
- tonnage: 32-39, 000 t.
- main armament: 9 x 28 cm + 8 x 12 cm + 14 x 10.5 cm Flak.
- speed: 32 knot
- range: 10,000 nautical miles at 19 nm/h.
- crew: 1,800 men.

● *Bismarck*

1935 budget laid down in 10.36 at Hamburg, launched 14.2.39, in service 24.8.40.

● *Tirpitz*

1936 budget laid down in 10.36, at Wilhelmshaven launched, 1.4.39, in service 25.2.41.

CHARACTERISTICS
- tonnage: 42-51/43-53, 000 t.
- main armament: 8 x 38 cm + 12 x 15 cm.
- speed: 31 knots + 16 x 10.5 cm Flak.
- crew: 2,530 range: 9,000 nautical miles at 19 nm/h.

HEAVY CRUISERS *SCHWERE KREUZER*

● *Admiral Hipper*

1935 budget laid down at Hamburg on 18.1.35, launched 6.2.37, in service 30.4.39.

● *Prinz Eugen*

1936 budget laid down at Kiel on 1.4.36, launched 22.8.38, in service 1.8.40.

● *Blücher*

1936 budget laid down at Kiel in 1936 launched 8.6.37 in service 20.9.39.

● *Seydlitz*

1937 budget laid down at Bremen on 9.10.36 launched 19.1.39, never completed.

CHARACTERISTICS
- tonnage: 14-19/15-20, 000 t.
- main armament: 8 x 20.3 cm + 12 x 10.5 cm Flak.
- speed: 31 knots range: 7,000 nautical miles at 19 nm/h.
- crew: 1,600 men.

LIGHT CRUISERS *LEICHTE KREUZER*

● *Königsberg*

1925 budget laid down in 1925 at Wilhelmshaven, launched 26.3.27, in service 17.4.29.

● *Karlsruhe*

1926 budget laid down in 1926 at Kiel launched 20.8.27 in service 6.11.29.

● *Köln*

1926 budget laid down in 1926 at Wilhelmshaven, launched 23.5.28, in service 15.1.30.

● *Leipzig*

1928 budget laid down in 4.28 at Wilhelmshaven, launched 18.10.29, in service 8.10.31.

● *Nürnberg*

1933 budget laid down 1933 at Kiel, launched 8.12.34, in service 2.11.35.

CHARACTERISTICS
- tonnage: 7/8,000 t
- main armament: 9 x 15 cm + 6 x 8.8 cm Flak.
- speed: 32 knots range: 5,000 nautical miles at 19 nm/h.
- crew: 850 men.

DESTROYERS *ZERSTÖRER*

1934 budget laid down at Kiel, in 1934, launched 1935/36.

● *Leberecht Maas* (Z 1) in service on 14.1.37.

● *Georg Thiele* (Z 2) in service on 27.2.37, laid down at Bremen in 1934 launched in 1935.

● *Paul Jacobi* (Z 5) in service on 29.6.37.

● *Theodor Riedel* (Z 6) in service on 26.7.37, laid down at Kiel in 1934, launched 1936/37.

● *Wolfgang Zenker* (Z 9) in service on 2.7.38.

● *Hans Lody* (Z 10) in service on 17.9.38. 1935 budget, laid down at Kiel in 1935, launched 1935/36.

● *Max Schultz* (Z 3) in service on 8.4.37.

● *Richard Beitzen* (Z 4) in service on 13.5.37, laid down at Bremen in 1935, launched in 1935.

● *Hermann Schoemann* (Z 7) in service on 15.9.37

● *Bruno Heinemann* (Z 8) in service on 8.1.38, laid down at Kiel in 1935, launched in 1937.

● *Bernd von Arnim* (Z 11) in service on 6.12.38.

● *Erich Giese* (Z 12) in service on 4.3.39.

● *Erich Koellner* (Z 13) in service on 15.8.39, laid down at Hamburg in 1935, launched in 1936/37.

● *Friedrich Ihn* (Z 14) in service on 9.4.38.

● *Erich Steinbrinck* (Z 15) in service on 8.6.38.

● *Friedrich Eckoldt* (Z 16) in service on 2.8.38, 1936 budget, laid down at Bremen in 1936, launched 1937.

● *Diether von Roeder* (Z 17) in service on 29.8.38

● *Hans Lüdemann* (Z 18) in service on 8.10.38.

● *Hermann Künne* (Z 19) launched 1937/38, in service on 12.1.39.

● *Karl Galster* (Z 20) launched in 1938 in service on 21.3.39.

- **Wilhelm Heidkamp** (Z 21) launched 1937/38, in service on 10.6.39.
- **Anton Schmitt** (Z 22) launched 1937/38, in service on 24.9.39.

CHARACTERISTICS
- **tonnage:** 2,300/3,200 t.
- **main armament:** 5 x 12.7 cm.
- **speed:** 38 knots.
- **range:** 4,400 nautical miles 19 nm/h.
- **crew:** 315 men.

TORPEDO BOATS
TORPEDOBOOTE

Type 1923 or Möwe class
Built in Wilhelmshaven.
- **Möwe** launched 3.26
- **Albatros, Greif, Seeadler**, launched 7.26
- **Falke, Kondor**, launched 9.26

CHARACTERISTICS
- **tonnage:** 920/1,290 t.
- **main armament:** 3 x 10.5 cm.
- **speed:** 33 knots.
- **range:** 2,000 nautical miles at 20 nm/h.
- **crew:** 75 men.
Conforming to the clauses of the Treaty of Versailles authorising twelve torpedo boats and twelve destroyers, a first series of twelve destroyers was laid down in 1923.

600 t T SERIES
1935 budget. 8 built in Elbing

- **T 1** put into service on 2.12.39.
- **T 2** put into service on 9.12.39.
- **T 3** put into service on 9.2.40.
- **T 4** put into service on 18.12.39.
4 built in Bremen
- **T 5** put into service on 23.1.40.
- **T 6** put into service on 30.4.40.
- **T 7** put into service on 20.12.39.
- **T 8** put into service on 28.10.39.

CHARACTERISTICS
- **tonnage:** 845/1,090 t
- **main armament:** 1 x 10.5 cm, 2 x 3 torpedo launchers.
- **speed:** 36 nautical miles range: 2,400 nautical miles at 19 nm/h.
- **crew:** 119 men.

SUBMARINES
UNTERSEEBOOTE
TYPE I A
1935-36 program
Submarines built in Bremen in 1935/36.
- **U 25** put into service on 6.4.36.
- **U 26** put into service on 11.5.36.

CHARACTERISTICS
- **tonnage:** 860 t
- **main armament:** 6 x 53.3 cm torpedo tubes
- **speed:** 18/8 knots.
- **range:** 6,700 nautical miles at 12 nm/h
- **crew:** 43 men

Type II A
1935-36 program
Coastal submarines built in Kiel (*Deutsche Weke*) in 1934/35.
- **U 1** to **U 6** brought into service beginning in June 1935.

CHARACTERISTICS
- **tonnage:** 250 t.
- **main armament:** 3 x 53.3 cm torpedo tubes.
- **speed:** 13/7 knots.
- **range:** 1, nautical miles at 12 nm/h.
- **crew:** 25 men.

TYPE II B
1935-36 program
Coastal submarines built in Kiel (Germania-Werft) starting in June 1935
- **U 7** put into service on 16.12.35
- **U 8** put into service on 13.8.35
- **U 9** 2.8.35
- **U 10** 1.9.35
- **U 11** 21.9.35
- **U 12** 21.10.35
built in Kiel (Deutsche Werke).
- **U 13** put into service on 21.10.35

- **U 14** put into service on 16.12.35.
- **U 15** in 1935 or 36
- **U 16** in 1935 or 36.
- **U 17** on 21.10.35.
built in Kiel (Germania-Werft) between 1935 and 1940.
- **U 18** put into service on 6.12.35
- **U 19** put into service on 23.12.35.
- **U 20** on 21.12.35.
1936-37 program, built in Kiel (Germania-Werft) between 1935 and 1940 put into service in 1936.
- **U 21** to **U 24**.

CHARACTERISTICS
- **tonnage:** 250 t
- **main armament:** 3 x 53.3 cm torpedo tubes
- **speed:** 13/7 knots
- **range:** 1,800 nautical miles at 12 nm/h
- **crew:** 25 men

- **TYPE VII A**
Coastal submarines built in Bremen between 1935 and 1937
- **U 27** put into service on 12.8.36
- **U 28** put into service on 1936.
- **U 29** in 1936
- **U 30** on 6.10.36.
- **U 31** on 28.12.36

- **U 32** in 1937.
- **U 33** in 1936, built in Kiel (Germania-Werft) between 1936 and 1937.
- **U 34** put into service on 12.9.36
- **U 35** put into service on 3.11.38.
- **U 36** on 16.12.36.

CHARACTERISTICS
- **tonnage:** 625 t.
- **main armament:** 5 x 53.3 cm torpedo tubes.
- **speed:** 16/8 knots
- **range:** 4,300 nautical miles at 12 nm/h.
- **crew:** 43 men.

RAPID FLEET ESCORTS
SCHNELLE FLOTTENBEGLEITER
Built between 1934 and 1936, these modern and extremely rapid escort vessels were intended for use as minesweepers and submarine hunters with large and rapid naval forces.

CHARACTERISTICS
- **tonnage:** 830 t.
- **main armament:** 2 x 10.5 cm.
- **speed:** 18/8 knots.
- **range:** 1,500 nautical miles at 20 nm/h.
- **crew:** 121 men.

The pocket battleship *Admiral Graf Spee.*

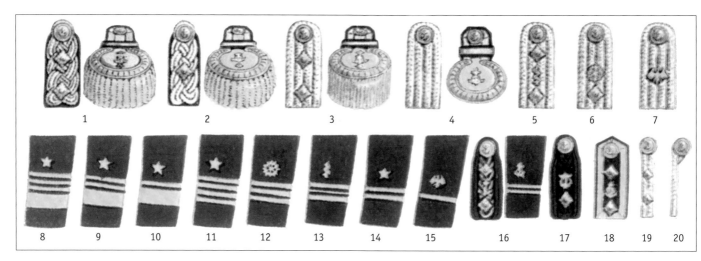

Rank insignia
1. Admiral
2. Commander
3. Lieutenant
4. Ensign
5. Doctor
6. Mechanic
7. Purser
8. Admiral
9. Vice-admiral
10. Rear-admiral
11. Commander and captain
12. Lieutenant-commander (mechanic)
13. Doctor captain
14. Sub-lieutenant
15. Ensign (purser)
16. Senior bridge officer
17. Bandmaster
18. First master
19. Midshipman (1st class)
20. Midshipman (2nd class)

— Two 10,000-tonne cruisers armed with eight 200 mm guns (pocket cruisers)

— Sixteen 1,625-tonne destroyers armed with five 127 mm guns

— Twenty 250-tonne submarines

— Six 500-tonne submarines

— Two 750-tonne submarines

— Ten 600-tonne escort vessels.

But in fact, most of these ships had already been laid down before the official publication of the program.

The situation on 1 January 1936 was as follows:

— Fifteen 250-tonne submarines and a 10,000-tonne heavy cruiser (Deutschland) were completed and in service

— a 10,000-tonne heavy cruiser (*Graf Spee*), a 6,000-tonne cruiser (Nuremberg) and a 2,600-tonne advice boat (*Grille*) were built.

As for officer recruitment, the schools could not supply enough men and like the army, called upon reserve officers (*Ergänzungs Offiziere*).

The navy did not have its own air arm and all of the aerial units stationed on the coastlines belonged to the Kiel Luftkreis, that fell under the command, as did the others, of the commander-in-chief of the air force. These aerial units flew for the navy, but could be called upon to take part in land operations.

The use of new weaponry and liaison between surface ships and submarines had been forbidden up that point and required a great amount of training. Also, German ships had to train to serve not only in the narrow European seas, but also in the ocean.

Manpower at this point was approximately 32,000 men, almost twice what was allowed by the Treaty of Versailles.

A big recruiting drive was undertaken. In order to train men for the crews of the high seas fleet, it was only possible to enlist for long periods of time. Some of the recruits that hailed from the coastal population were also seen as suitable for naval service.

Last of all, a 'pocket battleship' was put into service in 1933, with a third in 1935, as well as seventeen submarines in 1936, two heavy cruisers and seven destroyers in 1937. The naval forces and land based navy units (four coastal artillery groups, naval engineers, signals) were com-

1

AVIATION
1. Flag of the *Reich* transport aviation
NAVY
2. War pennant
3. Vice admiral insignia
4. Old imperial war pennant (replaced 31 May 1934)
5. Rear admiral insignia
6. Admiral insignia
7. Pilot flag
8. Squadron commander pennant

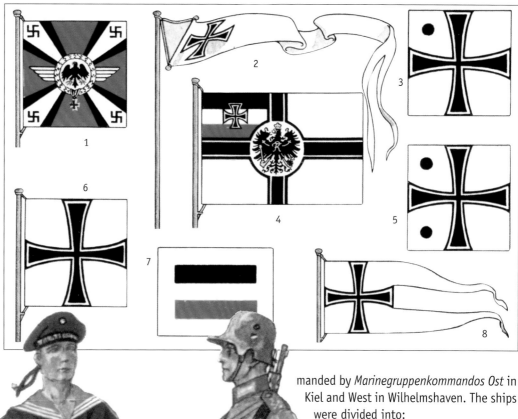

1. Petty officer
2. 1st class quarter-master radio operator
3. Rating
4. Shore-based rating

2   3   4

manded by *Marinegruppenkommandos Ost* in Kiel and West in Wilhelmshaven. The ships were divided into:

• the naval line division comprising five battleships with one in reserve.

• pathfinder naval forces with six cruisers, sixteen torpedo boats, minesweepers and submarines.

When they entered into service, the torpedo boats came under the command of the torpedo boat commander (*Führer der Torpedoboote*) at Swinemünde, a position created in September 1933 to command torpedo boats and fast launches.

The *Kriegsmarine* was in full expansion and the naval shipyards were working at full capacity. It was, however, still far from being the 'balanced navy' that the admirals wished to have. They were still lacking capital ships, the remainder of the submarines and above all, destroyers and escort vessels.

DIE LUFTWAFFE

The clauses of the Treaty of Versailles stipulated that Germany was forbidden any kind of military air force. However, thanks to the tireless and secret activity of the various governments that existed between 1926 and 1932, more or less parallel institutions were progressively given the means to rapidly renovate the German air force.

When Hitler came to power, the following was already in place:

— design and research sections at the *Reichswehr* ministry
— a core of military aviators within the armed services
— a partially militarised sporting and commercial aviation
— a powerful aeronautical industry that was capable of rapidly manufacturing military aircraft

THE CREATION OF THE LUFTWAFFE

The development of the future *Luftwaffe* was therefore carried out in secret, initially under the cover of Lufthansa whose transport aircraft, notably the Junkers 52, could be transformed into bombers. The civilian air company trained future combat pilots and showed them night navigation techniques.

Also, between 1924 and 1933, the Soviet Union, whose assistance had been requested, placed a training airfield near Lipetsk at the disposal of German pilots where they were able to fly modern Dutch, Russian and finally, German aircraft.

A large financial assistance was also given to sporting clubs for flying gliders or motor-powered aircraft, thus forming a pool of future *Luftwaffe* fighter pilots.

Finally, the Air Ministry (*Reichsminister der Luftfahrt* or RLM) created on 5 May 1933, made a great effort in creating the necessary infrastructure (airfields, hangars, workshops), and aeronautical construction and training.

1. *Kettenführer* (German air navigation school)
2. *Flugzeugführer (*German aerial sport association)
RANK INSIGNIA
3. *Flieger*
4. *Oberflieger*
5. *Hilfsflugzeugführer*
6. *2. Flugzeugführer*
7. *1. Flugzeugführer*
8. *Unterflugmeister*
9. *Flugmeister*
10. *Oberflugmeister*
11. *Kettenführer*
12. *Schwarmführer*
13. *Fliegerkapitän*
14. *Fliegerkommandant*
15. *Flieger-Vizekommodore*
16. *Fliegerkommodore*
17. *Staatssekretär*
18. Minister
Collar tabs were light blue for the *Deutscher Luftsportverband*, yellow for the *Deutsche Verkehrsfliegerschule*, black for the *Reichsluftfahrtministerium* and white for the minister and state secretary.

These precious elements thus allowed the new leadership to create, an air force and a reserve, as early as 1934.

German aerial rearmament began at the end of 1933 and continued in secret the following year. In the spring of 1934, the rearmament program set itself the objective of creating, for October 1936, a first line air force comprising six bomber and two fighter wings, eleven (independent) reconnaissance squadrons and ten (cooperation) reconnaissance squadrons, making 93 squadrons with approximately 1,400 aircraft.

The creation of the *Luftwaffe* and the nomination of Hermann Goering as its commander-in-chief (*Oberbefehlshaber der Luftwaffe*) were divulged in February 1935. Goering, both aviation minister and commander of air forces, played an essential and determining role in its rise. He worked tirelessly and publicly declared that Germany would go to any lengths in order to have an air force worthy of the name.

In the spring of 1935, the results achieved were such that all the careful concealment that had been in place up to that point was partially abandoned. Indeed, on 10 March 1935, six days before the signing of the decree establishing the *Wehrmacht*, Goering announced the official creation of an air force, the parity of which with the Royal Air Force (approximately 1,000 aircraft) was recognised a few days later by Hitler.

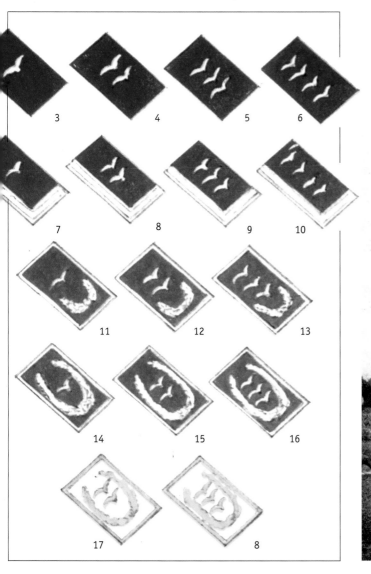

A 2 cm wheeled anti-aircraft gun.

The 21 May military law mentioned that the *Luftwaffe* was part of the *Wehrmacht*. It placed all of units who may have a role to play in aerial operations under the authority of the Commander-in-Chief of the air force.

MILITARY AVIATION

The air force was created by the merger of the *Reichswehr* and civil aviation personnel.

It initially comprised:

— a naval air arm whose main centres were situated at Kiel-Holtenau, List on the island of Sylt, Rostock and Warnemünde

— a ground-based air force with 700 modern combat aircraft, still carefully concealed, with a majority of bombers, organised territorially into aerial districts with bases, airports and parks.

The ground-based air force was created with:

— an aerial fleet (bomber, fighter and reconnaissance units) placed under the orders of a command set up in Berlin

— a cooperation air force (reconnaissance and observation units)

— training centres working flat out at Brunswick, Cottbus, Döberitz, Gotha, Jüterbog and Schleissheim near Munich.

Six aerial districts (Luftkreise) were established on 1 April 1934:

- *Luftkreis I* at Königsberg
- *Luftkreis II* at Berlin
- *Luftkreis III* at Dresden
- *Luftkreis IV* at Münster
- *Luftkreis V* at Munich
- *Luftkreis VI* at Kiel (for the naval air arm)

At the beginning of 1936, bombers made up 60% of the ground air force strength, with:

• twelve 'heavy' bomber groups equipped with the Junkers 52 and Dornier Do 23.

• a dive-bomber group equipped with the Heinkel He 50.

Fighter aircraft made up 20% of the strength with five groups equipped with the Heinkel He 51 and forming *Jagdgeschwader* 132 "*Richthofen*" created at Döberitz on 14 March 1935 and *Jagdgeschwader* 134 "*Horst Wessel*" created the following year.

Reconnaissance units represented 20% of the ground air force strength, of which only 10% cooperated with the army. The latter, relatively low number, would probably be rectified upon mobilisation of what the *Luftwaffenreserve* could provide with reserves.

Adolf Hitler observes a 8.8 cm gun anti-aircraft telemeter in use.

LUFTWAFFE MATERIEL

The first aircraft were civil planes converted into bombers in 1925, or planes that had been designed for this role, but which were deemed unsatisfactory. After a shaky start, the Dornier Do 23 was finally tested in September 1934 and two years later, 240 F and G types were in service with the Luftwaffe. Also, Junkers was asked to transform its three-engine Ju 52 transport plane into an 'improvised bomber'. This therefore created the 'first auxiliary bomber group' under the aegis of Lufthansa with eighty Ju 52. Kampfgeschwader 154 was then formed, followed on 15 March 1936 by KG 152.

At the same time, Junkers began looking at a twin-engine plane for both civilian transport and as a bomber, the prototype of which undertook its maiden flight in November 1934. The first Ju 86 were delivered to the Luftwaffe during the summer of 1936. A similar Dornier project, but this time for a postal plane, led to the Do 17 with production beginning in May 1934. The two latter aircraft were still biplanes with a tubular wood and metal structure covered with fabric. They were armed with two MG 17 and, following tests at Lipetsk, five to six-bomb capacity racks for attacking infantry. Particularly easy to fly, the Arado 65 was built in great numbers and flew as a training aircraft until 1933. As for the HD 49, it disappointed, despite its aerodynamics. After a disappointing maiden flight in November 1932, a modified aircraft, named the HD 51, was presented during the course of the summer of 1933 and the Luftwaffe began to receive them starting in 1935.

The first Arado Ar 68 was built in the summer of 1933 with the same BMW engine as the He 51. Although the two planes had more or less the same power output, the AR 68 was chosen in 1936 to equip fighter units, following test flights with both aircraft by the fighter ace and test pilot Ernst Udet. At the same time, a training plane was needed for training beginner pilots, and Arado, Focke-Wulf, Heinkel and Henschel competed to present a single-seater plane for putting the final touches to fighter pilot training. It was the Arado 76 with its metal structure that was finally retained.

In December 1933, the technical services saw the need for an all-metal single-seater interceptor, with a single wing and retractable undercarriage. In February 1934, Arado, Heinkel and Bayerische Flugzeugwerke began looking at such a project. The prototypes carried out their first flights in 1934: July for the Arado Ar 80, October for the Heinkel He 112 and Messerschmitt Bf 109.

December 1933 also saw the design of a heavy twin-engine fighter named Zerstörer. The Focke-Wulf 187, designed by Kurt Tank, was a twin-engine single-seater plane armed with two MG 17. As the RLM had not given any specifications for this type of aircraft, Tank got in touch with and obtained &a contract from *General* Wolfram von Richthofen, the head of the technical bureau at the ministry, in the winter of 1935. The first prototype was built in December 1936 and undertook its maiden flight in April of the following year.

At the same time, Messerschmitt put forward a design for its Bf 110, a twin-engine aircraft that was faster than the Bf 109 and armed with four MG 17. Its maiden flight was in May 1936 and a first production run started at the beginning of the following year.

- Arado Ar 64
- Arado Ar 65
- Arado Ar 6
- Arado Ar 68
- Arado Ar 76
- Arado Ar 80
- Dornier Do 23
- Focke-Wulf Fw 56
- Focke-Wulf Fw 187
- Heinkel HD 43
- Heinkel He 45
- Heinkel He 46
- Heinkel HD 49
- Heinkel He 50
- Heinkel He 51
- Heinkel He 74
- Heinkel He 112
- Henschel Hs 121
- Henschel Hs 125
- Junkers Ju 52
- Messerschmitt Bf 109
- Messerschmitte Bf 110
- Junkers Ju 52
- Dornier Do 23
- Heinkel He 50
- Heinkel He 51
- Heinkel He 45
- Heinkel He 46

It comprised:

• three independent reconnaissance squadrons equipped with the Heinkel He 45 and 46.

• three army cooperation squadrons like the independent reconnaissance squadrons.

Although the naval air arm comprising a dozen squadrons and a dozen seaplane bases remained at the disposal of the navy, it remained under the authority of the *Luftwaffe* commander-in-chief.

GENERAL AVIATION RESERVE

The aviation reserves were formed thanks to the militarization of civil and sporting aviation. Organised and trained militarily, they were in full development and capable of putting 1,500 aircraft into action.

Lufthansa was the world's biggest air company and held the monopoly on all commercial air activity in the Reich. It had a hundred transformable civil aircraft and three hundred crews experienced in all types of mission. It was thus ready to operate in the event of mobilisation.

Under the direct authority of the *Luftwaffe* commander-in-chief, it appeared to be capable of creating an auxiliary bomber fleet of 18 squadrons for a total of 270 aircraft.

In peacetime, six of these squadrons equipped with air force aircraft were used for the military training of Lufthansa personnel.

The *Luftwaffen*reserve was also placed under the command of the air force commander-in-chief via the German association for aerial sports (Deutscher Luftsportverband or DLV). The role of the latter, via its civil aviation school (*Zentrale Verkehrs Fliegerschule or ZVF*), was to take over some of the air force's training workload by providing full pilot training with, and military flying training for men who had not undertaken obligatory military service (23 to 32), while main-

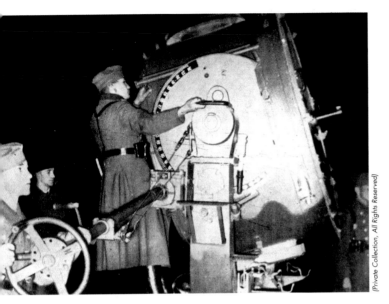

A 130 mm diameter Flak searchlight.

LUFTWAFFE GUNS

● Automatic 3.7 cm M Flak 18, rate of fire 150 rounds per minute, vertical range 5,000 m
● 7.5 cm Flak 14, modified old materiel due to be progressively phased out.
● 8.8 cm Flak 18, rate of fire 15-20 rounds per minute, maximum vertical range approximately 10,000 m, effective range approximately 7,000 m

fifteen aerial regions (*Landesgruppen*). These regions were divided into local aviation groups (*Fliegergruppen*) with a certain number of squadrons (*Fliegerstürme*) some of which had seven to nine aircraft served by approximately ninety men. It would have the capability, once it had received the appropriate materiel, of forming ninety squadrons with twelve aircraft each.

taining the training level for air force reservists.

With this structure and way of functioning, it constituted a considerable force that in the event of war could immediately increase the power of the *Luftwaffe* by:

— compensating losses suffered by active units
— allowing the formation of new units
— topping up personnel of the observation squadrons necessary to the air force.

With a strength of 50,000 members, of which 3,500 - 4,000 were well-trained pilots, the DLV was divided up into

ANTI-AIRCRAFT DEFENCE

The *Flak-Abwehr-Korps* (Flak) comprised a few regiments with:

— two heavy groups with three batteries of 8.8 cm guns, a 3.7 cm automatic gun battery
— a light group armed with 2 cm heavy machine-guns and 3.7 cm guns
— a searchlight group with two 150 cm searchlights (intended for heavy Flak groups), a 60 cm searchlight (intended for light Flak groups) and four-horn listening devices intended for heavy groups.

Arado Ar96.

At the end of 1935, the *Luftwaffe* had 2,000 aircraft, 800 of which were for combat purposes. In fact, these were first generation aircraft that were in no way superior to planes in the British, French or Italian service.

Territorial organisation put into place beginning with the creation, on 1 April 1934, of the Landkreise II and Vinat Berlin and Munich, followed by the I in Königsberg, the III in Dresden, the IV in Münster and the VI in Kiel for the Baltic and North Sea front.

In all probability, forecasts were achieved six months in advance. We might even believe that, since the projects were elaborated, they were expanded (infrastructure going

Focke Wulf FW 56 Stösser in flight.

beyond the original program: a monthly production rate of 200 planes since April 1934). This might signify that this was a first stage and that another would follow soon after.

Whatever the prospects, the German air forces began to make their presence felt in European forces.

Here again, the obvious problem is still the same: the rapid reconstruction of forces had outstripped the training of its officers and NCOs, making it highly probable that serious difficulties were experienced in this area.

2 cm anti-aircraft gun on a pivot mount.

THE POLICE

When Adolf Hitler took power *(die Machtübernahme)*, there was authority controlling all of the police units within Germany. The country was divided into several administrative provinces or regions *(Länder)* hailing from the monarchy period and retained by the Weimar Republic.

There were five main Länder with a regional government:
• *Land Preussen,* regrouping Berlin, Thuringia, Oldenburg and the Hanseatic town of Bremen, Prussian Saxony and Hesse-Nassau.
• *Land Bayern,* comprising of Bavaria and Bavarian Rhineland-Palatinate.

• *Land Sachsen* or the former territory of the kingdom of Saxony.
• *Land Baden* or the former territory of the Grand Duchy of Baden.
• *Land Württemberg.*
The arrival of the Nazis in January 1933 led to a pro-

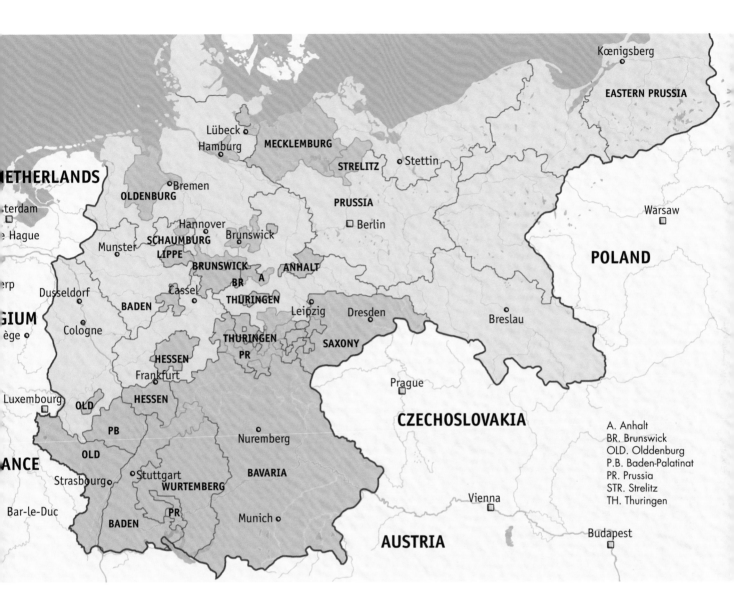

A 1934 map of Germany showing its main administrative subdivisions.

found change in police structures, following those of the Prussian police, and an increasing centralisation. In the space of three years they formed a disciplined machine whose main role was to keep the German people under the control of the National Socialist Party.

The evolution of the police was also marked by an increasing militarization as, despite the constant increase in permanent regular forces, the leaders of the Reich wanted to retain auxiliary armed forces capable at all times of carrying out missions usually given to regular units. This was in order to compensate for legal means, if need be.

THE NAZIS AND THE POLICE

Initially there was no authority with the overall command of the various police forces and their poorly defined organisation. Although the constitution allowed the Reich home secretary to exercise financial control over police units, each *Land* jealously guarded control in order to preserve autonomy and traditions. The regional police forces were mostly independent of the others and had no defined connections. They had their own administrative and pay systems, uniforms and even judicial code.

Neither the Treaty of Versailles nor the Weimar Republic modified the provincial nature of the German police, even though the constitution stated that financial control could be exercised by the Reich home secretary. Thus, by refusing to approve the allocation of funds for a provincial police force, the ministry had some measure of control.

In any case, the *Länder* continued the administration of their police forces. For the Nazis to achieve their goals however, they needed a common administration and powerful police forces that were united and tightly controlled by a central government. The first few months following Hitler's taking of power were dedicated to assimilating and coordinating (*Gleichshaltung*) all organisations in conformity with the changes that had taken place in the government of the Reich itself.

The first attempts at unification came up against the opposition of the provinces, in particular catholic Bavaria that was traditionally opposed to any attempt by protestant Prussia to take away its rights. The Nazis, therefore, began by taking over the provincial governments.

They then forced out any police personnel that they suspected of being republican or democratic sympathisers, replacing them with *Alte Kämpfer*, the 'old fighters' of the Nazi movement whose loyalty could not be doubted in any way. The first big change undertaken within the police forces was in the domain of political police (*Politische Polizei*), known in Prussia as *Staatspolizei* or *Stapo* and whose budget had been greatly reduced during the Weimar Republic period.

As soon as they came to power, the Nazis created a secret state police force that had not existed under either the Empire or the Republic. Prussia, the largest and most military of all the provinces, with Hermann Goering as prime minister, led the way on 26 April 1933 by replacing the former Prussian political police with the *Geheime Staatspolizei* (secret state police).

At the same time, Heinrich Himmler, Reichsführer SS, acquired official nominations. He was named as police prefect for Munich and chief of the Bavarian police. Then, in November 1933, his powers were extended to all of the Reich police forces, with the exception of Prussia where Göering was the master, and supported by the *Gestapo* that he had just created.

On 10 April 1934, two months before the 'night of the long knives', Himmler ousted Goering, who was busy forming 'his' Luftwaffe, and took control of the Gestapo.

TOWARDS CENTRALISATION

A first step towards centralised control was taken on 30 January 1934 when the decree concerning the reconstruction of the Reich was published (*Gesetz über den neu Aufbau des Reiches*), stating that the sovereign rights of the provinces were now transferred to the Reich as were, therefore, the police forces of each province. In fact, this decree did not change much in the every day routine of the police forces.

Then, on 2 February, a new decree stated that the sovereign rights transferred to the Reich would remain in the hands of the Länder who would act by central government delegation in all cases that were not of interest to the latter. Although the provinces retained their own control, the real power in fact was exercised from Berlin, with the central government retaining the option of absorbing police

1   2

duties. It was this freedom of choice that was responsible for the complicated structure of the German police system and its abnormal way of functioning.

THE *LANDESPOLIZEI* AND GOERING REGIMENT

The next step was unification and centralisation (*Verreichlichung*) of the police and the creation of a militarised police (*Kasernierte Landespolizei*) trained and equipped like infantry.

Prussia had already led the way in this domain. With the decree of 26 March 1933, it had established a certain

1. Police general
2. *Polizeiabteilung z.b.V. Wecke*
3. *Polizeioberwachtmeister*
4. Mounted policeman

The new standard of the Berlin police and its guard parade through the streets of the German capital.

number of inspectorates (*Landespolizei-Inspektionen*) tasked with *'preparing and carrying out defensive measures against internal unrest'*. Prussia's example was rapidly followed by the other *Länder* and on 29 March 1935 all administration was taken over by the Reich home office and finance ministry. Then, two days later, it was decreed that all of the police forces came under central government control.

The Reich home secretary now controlled the eleven regions (*Landspolizei Inspektionen*) that were placed under the orders of police generals who had mostly served in the old army and had at their disposal a staff comparable to that of an infantry division.

They consisted of units analogous to regiments and battalions with specialist formations: machine-guns, motorcyclists, turret-less armoured cars, signals, engineers, aircraft. They received *Reichswehr* training, and the autumn

The new police flags parade in Nuremberg.

manoeuvres that it carried out along the border zones were the same as those of the army.

The only thing missing in order for a police region to be comparable to a *Reichsheer* division was divisional artillery. Indeed, grouped under a centralised command were:
— the strength of a divisional infantry
— the strength of a cavalry regiment
— an engineers unit and a signals detachment.

It is clear that in the areas near the eastern border, that these units could form the bulk of covering forces.

In 1934-35, the Landespolizei forces, now with a strength of 4,000 officers and 100,000 men, were grouped together along the Rhine and in a fifty kilometre strip east of the river, no doubt as a covering force for the army. However, it was during the course of 1935 that the purely military character of the *Lapo* became obvious. As each as 10 March, when obligatory military service was brought back, the *Landespolizei* homeland inspectorates, outside of the demilitarised zone, came under the direct command of the War Ministry, whereas the three inspectorates of the demilitarised zone and their 30,000 men remained attached to the Home Office.

On 3 July 1935, a law decreed the transfer to the *Wehrmacht* of the forces of the eight as of inspectorates, disbanded on 1 August and 50,000 policemen and 2,000 officers became professional soldiers, forming a useful core of well-trained and disciplined soldiers. Then, on 7 March 1936, it only took an order for the three forces of the three remaining inspectorates in the demilitarised zone to join the other previously mentioned units, with the exception of the Göering Regiment.

The origins of this unit can be found in the *Schutzpolizeiabteilung zur besondere Verwendung*, a special security detachment under the command of a police officer named Wecke and formed with carefully selected police officers. On becoming a regiment, it was stationed in Berlin and was the praetorian guard of the Air Ministry. With the new military law, it began receiving recruits like an ordinary infantry regiment on 1 October 1935. It was, in reality, a veritable motorised infantry regiment. After 7 March 1936, it was the only unit to retain its uniform and name of a police regiment.

THE *SCHUTZPOLIZEI*

The Nazis next focused their attention on the municipal police forces (*Gemeindepolizei*) that were often organised differently according to the province or the town.

Prussia once more led the way by giving its municipal police provincial status. Then, on 25 October 1935, the Reich and Prussian home office imposed various rules that now dictated the administration of the municipal police. A municipal police chief was named with the role of standardising and commanding the activities of the municipal police within the various towns of the Reich.

Then, on 24 June 1935, as stipulated by the law concerning German police, the police received the nomenclature of 'municipal protection police' (*Schutzpolizei der Gemeinden*) which was then merged with the *Schutzpolizei des Reiches*. In large conurbations, the municipal police forces were grouped together into a *Kommando der Schutzpolizei* led by a commander in the Schutzpolizeidienstabteilung under the orders of a captain or lieutenant.

The *Schutzpolizei* was the real police force of the Reich, along with the Gendarmerie and community police.

The Gendarmerie was a rural police force attached to communities of less fewer 2,000 inhabitants. The main difference with the *Schupo* was that, its personnel were in addition to their police role, trained and equipped to assist the population with administrative matters and relations with administrative authorities in general.

The *Schutzpolizei* was an urban police force with the organisation and role of an ordinary police force. Grouped together in

2

3

4

1. Bavarian provincial police
2. Saxon police
3. Württemberg police
   second lieutenant
4. Baden police

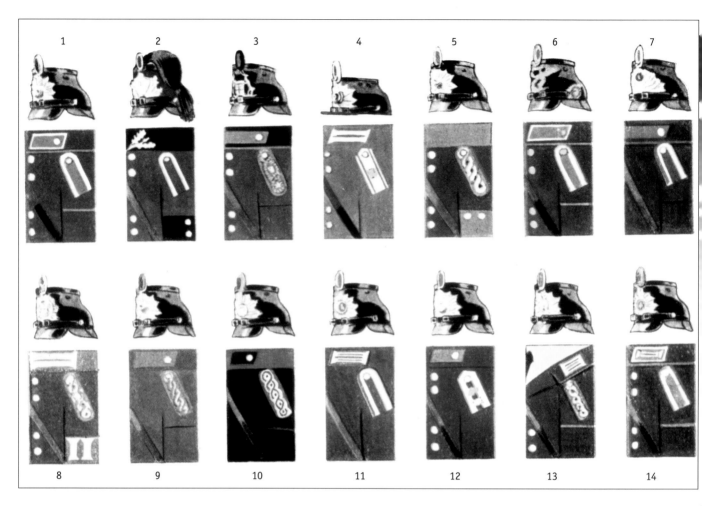

company-sized units, it constituted the shock force of the police and comprised:

- police stationed in barracks,
- Police not stationed in barracks working on an individual basis,
- The *Feldjägerkorps*.

Its manpower was increased beginning on 1 March 1935 with a certain amount of elements of the disbanded police inspectorates that were deemed unfit for *Wehrmacht* service.

The *Feldjägerkorps* was created in 1935 within the *Schutzpolizei* in order to ensure the policing within the National-Socialist Party. Formed into companies (*Bereitschaften*), they were equipped with motorised vehicles, constituting a barracks-based and militarised formation tasked with traffic control duties. Its units were placed in the demilitarised zone (2,000 men) in Berlin and the large industrial regions. Its total strength was approximately 7 to 8,000

HEADDRESS AND TUNICS
1. Prussian police
2. Bavarian provincial police
3. Württemberg police
4. Saxony police
5. Thuringia police
6. Baden police
7. Hessian police
8. Mecklenburg police
9. Oldenburg police
10. Brunswick police
11. Bremen police
12. Lubeck police
13. Hamburg police
14. Lippe police
15. Prussian police
16. Prussian communal police
17 and 18. Bavarian police
19. Saxony police
20. Württemberg police
21. Baden police
22. Mecklenburg police
23. Thuringia police
24. Brunswick police
25. Oldenburg police

26. Anhalt police
27. Bremen police
28. Lippe police
RANK INSIGNIA
29. *Polizei-Oberwachtmeister* (police schools and intervention units)
30. *Anwärter* (cadet)
31. *Polizei-Wachtmeister*
32. *Polizei-Wachtmeister* with more than 4 years of service
33. *Polizei-Oberwachtmeister*
34. *Polizei-Hauptwachtmeister*
35. *Polizei-Meister*
36. *Polizei-Obermeister*
37. *Leutnant* (second-lieutenant)
38. *Oberleutnant* (lieutenant)
39. *Hauptmann* (captain)
40. *Major* (major)
41. *Oberstleutnant* (lieutenant-colonel)
42. *Oberst* (colonel)
43. *General* (general)
44. *Polizei-Hauptwachtmeister*

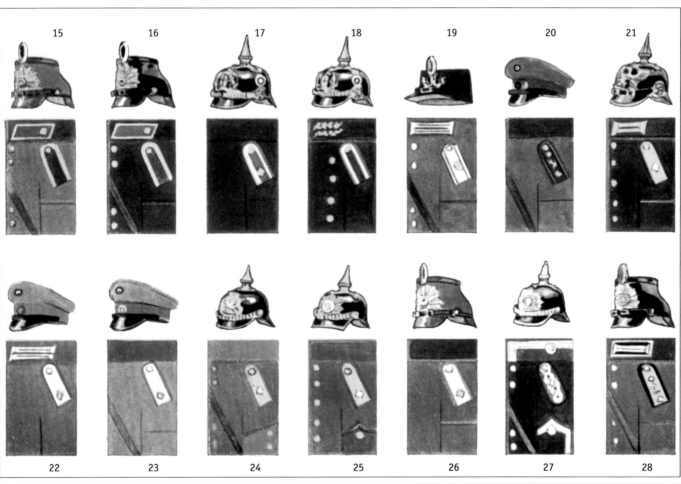

15 16 17 18 19 20 21

22 23 24 25 26 27 28

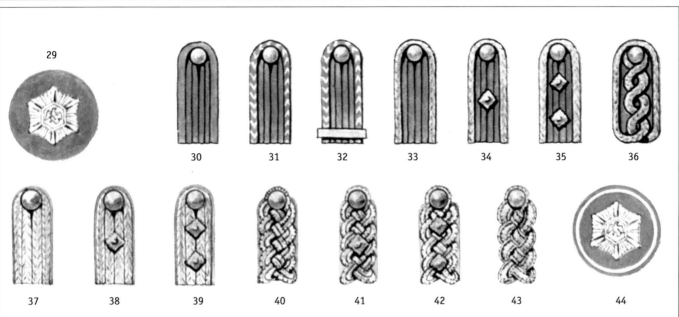

29

30 31 32 33 34 35 36

37 38 39 40 41 42 43 44

men, with recruits coming from the best SA elements. In the event of war, its units were capable of supplying road traffic detachments to the large motorised units.

Finally, other police personnel could play a military role. The railway police or *Bahnschutz* comprised of permanent elements or units that were formed in needed. In July 1935, they took part in guarding rail stations and bridges in the Kassel region during the Kyffhauser conference and the Nuremberg area in September 1935 for the Nazi Party congress. Their training had a military and technical character that meant they could, if war broke out, carry out tasks usually devolved to:

— lines of communication guards
— field railway platoons
— railway sapper units.

They received a four-week training course on the destruction and re-establishment of the lines of communication (bridges) and protection against air attacks.

THE COMPLETION OF CENTRALISATION

The process of centralisation was completed on 17 June 1935 with the creation of the position of Chief of the German Police (*Chef der deutschen Polizei*) at the Reich Interior Ministry, a position taken by Heinrich Himmler with the title of *Reichsführer SS und Chef der Deutschen Polizei im Reichsministerium des Innern*. As a member of the police, he was attached to the Interior Ministry, but as an SS man, he was under the direct command of Hitler, giving him a clear advantage over his minister.

On 26 June 1936, a decree stating the dividing of roles within the German police chief bureau (*Geschäftsverteilung im Geschäftbereich des Chefs der Deutschen Polizei*) saw Himmler divide the police into two main branches:

• The *Ordnungspolizei (Orpo)* or standard police led by SS

1. Thuringia *police*
2. Hessian police captain
3. Mecklenburg police
4. Hamburg police

1

2

3

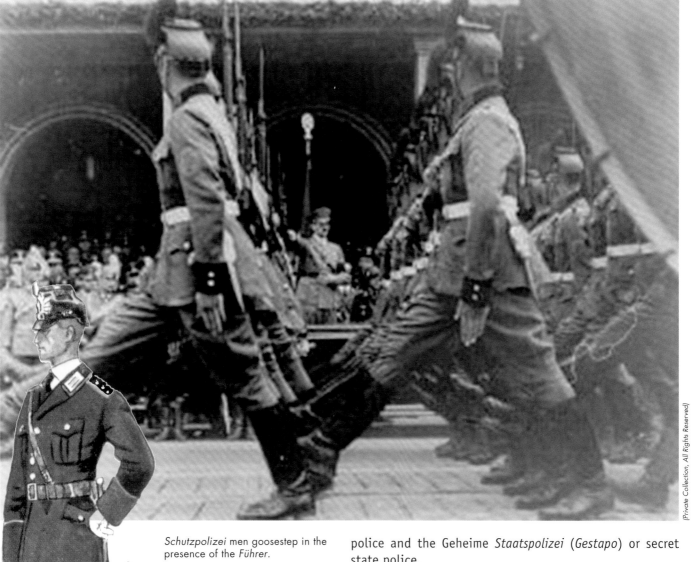

Schutzpolizei men goosestep in the presence of the *Führer*.

Obergruppenführer und Generaloberst der Polizei Kurt Daluege that grouped together the *Schutzpolizei* or urban police, the Gendarmerie or rural police, as well as the *Verwaltungspolizei* or administrative police.

• The *Sicherheitspolizei* (*Sipo*) or security police commanded by *SS-Gruppenführer* Reinhard Heydrich consisting of the *Reichskriminalpolizei* (*Kripo*) or criminal investigation police and the Geheime *Staatspolizei* (*Gestapo*) or secret state police.

Local or central police activity throughout the Reich was not disrupted by these innovations. However, the superficial character of local administration was accentuated by the nomination of certain high-ranking police civil servants tasked with supervising these regional Orpo or Sipo elements and ensuring liaison between local governments and central police services in Berlin.

Each of these military regions also hadan inspector for each branch. Designated by decree on 20 September 1936, they were tasked with cooperating with the NSDAP Gauleiter, the general commanding the military region, and with the administrative authorities of the region they were attached to.

4

Also, Himmler named three general Ordnungspolizei inspectors:

- for the urban police (*Der Generalinspekteur der Schutzpolizei des Reiches*)

- for the urban and municipal police (*Der Generalinspekteur der Gendarmerie und der Schutzpolizei der Gemeinden*)

- for police schools (*Der Generalinspekteur der Polizeischulen*).

The main task of these inspectors was to propose impro-

vements in the functioning of their respective services and more generally in ensuring prooper overall fuctionning.

Another step towards centralisation was undertaken on 25 June 1936 when the decision was made to equip all police forces with the same uniform and to adopt standardised badges and rank insignia.

1. Prussian police captain
2. Bavarian police
3. Württemberg police
4. Brunswick police

SPECIAL POLICE *(LANDJÄGEREI)*
5. Dantzig police
6. Bavarian *Schutzmannschaft*
7. *Feldjägerkorps*
8. Naval arsenal police

5   6   7   8

THE PARTY FORMATIONS

Adolf Hitler's adhesion to the *Deutsch Arbeiter-Partei* in September 1919, marked the beginning of a new movement. Named as party propaganda chief on 5 January 1920, he organised a gathering at the Hofbraühaus festival hall on 24 February.

In front of more than 2,000 people and an increasing enthusiasm, he covered the twenty-five points of the new party's program.

The movement gathered startling momentum and, on 21 April, the first group situated outside of Munich was formed in Rosenheim. Hitler modified the Party's name, to the *Nationalsozialistische Deutsche Arbeitpartei*, after having adopted a flag bearing the swastika.

On 17 December, Hitler purchased the *Völkischer Beo-*

Adolf Hitler seen here during the *Fahnenweihe,* the solemn and almost presentation of Nazi Party emblems.

bachter which became the official newspaper of the national-socialist movement. Then, on 21 January 1921, the Part, now with three thousand members, held its first general assembly.

Continuing its effort, the NSDAP constantly organised mass or group meetings that attracted increasing numbers

ORGANISATIONS

of listeners. Finally, on 21 July, Adolf Hitler was named as party president.

THE PARTY AND THE SA

The Nazi Party's main opponent was the Communist Party. Conflict between the two was inevitable. Hitler, therefore, decided to create a shock organisation: ' the sport and gymnastics association' on 3 August 1921. This was the beginning of militant groups tasked with maintaining order, forcibly if need be, during NSDAP demonstrations and meetings. The disbanding of the Free Corps the same month allowed to recruit from their ranks and to increase manpower.

The first serious confrontation between Nazis and Marxists took place on 4 November during a meeting held

at the Hofbraühaus. During the course of a violent fight, forty strong-arm men managed to rout eight hundred opponents. Hitler then decided to transform the sporting association into 'assault groups' or *Sturmabteilungen* (*SA*).

The growth of the NSDAP continued and, at the end of January 1922, the second assembly gathered six thousand members in Munich. S eeing that the struggle would become increasingly violent, Hitler then decided to strengthen the structure and manpower of the SA. The new units (*Standarte*) paraded for the first time in public on 16 August 1922.

The opportunity to use the SA in action came on 14 October during the 'German day' organised by the federa-

Party hierarchy
A. *Gauleiter*
B. *Blockwart*
1. *Blockwart* (housing block)
2. *Gauleiter* (province)
3. *Zellenwart* (cell)
4. *Landesinspektor*
5. *Ortsgruppenleiter* (group of localities)
8. *Reichsinspektor*
9. *Kreisleiter* (borough)
10. *Reichsorganisationsleiter*

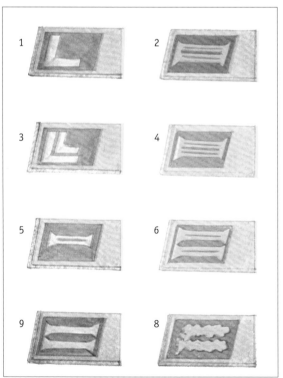

A   B

tion of nationalist parties. Hitler arrived in Coburg with his troops and gained the upper hand over the communist trade unionists that attempted to attack the SA and prevent the meeting.

Following the success of the Coburg expedition, SA membership reached 6,000 men in December 1922 and the last Bavarian communist areas were eliminated.

However, strength was still insufficient to play a major role in Germany. Hitler, therefore, decided:

1. to add to the SA units already formed outside the Party, including the *Reischsflagge* of Captain Rudolf Hess and the *Bund Oberland* of Dr Weber

2. to arm the *SA* with rifles and machine-guns

3. to proceed with the reorganisation of his forces with the role of commander-in-chief being conferred to the former pilot Captain Hermann Goering and Captain Ernst Röhm as chief-of-staff.

Following these transformations, the National-Socialist Party was forbidden in Prussia, Saxony, Thuringia, Baden and Mecklenburg. This led to many men heading to Munich and, therefore, increasing the Party's cohesion and dynamism. In March 1923, there were six thousand SA organised into four Standarte.

On 1 May 1923, nearly ten thousand armed Nazis paraded at the Oberwiesenfeld airfield near Munich. Following this demonstration, the SA attempted to march on the town, but were thwarted by regular soldiers. Despite this, Hitler succeeded in gathering 70,000 men in Nuremberg on 1-2 September, inspecting them on the Herrnwiese, with General Ludendorff participating in this 'German day'.

The NSDAP then allied itself more closely with armed right-wing units, forming with them the 'German Combat League' (*Deutscher Kampfbund*) with Hitler nominated as political chief on 25 September 1923. Their aim was to forge German unity via a dictatorship.

In Bavaria, the Kampfbund had an adversary in the form of the conservative party led by von Karr. The latter, having secured the support of General von Lessow, commander of *Wehrkreis VII*, proclaimed himself general state commissary for Bavaria on 26 September, claiming overall power.

Hitler was thus forced to take action once more and made the most of a meeting held on 8 November at the Munich Bürgerbräukeller de Munich by von Karr, in order to launch a surprise attack. However, after initial success, two thousand Nazis were surrounded by the Bavarian police. In an attempt to break out, they began marching towards the cordon formed by the police and infantrymen of the 19th Bavarian Regiment around the Odeonsplatz, next to the Feldherrnhalle. The clash was violent. Sixteen men were killed, five of whom were members of Hitler's *Stoßtrupp* Hitler, the bodyguard unit formed in May with students under the command of Rudolf Hess.

Hitler, wounded, was arrested, as were Ludendorff and Röhm; only Goering managed to get away. Sentenced to five years in prison on 26 February 1924, Hitler would go on to write '*Mein Kampf*'.

1. *Obergruppenführer*
2. *Brigadeführer* of the *Sachsen* Group
3. *Oberführer* of the *Rheinland* Group
4. *Standartenführer* of the *Bayerische Ostmark* Group

After these events, the bloodstained swastika flag was picked up by the police and handed back to the Party when they came to power, it became known as the Blutfahne, the 'bloody banner' and was present at all the important ceremonies. In the same way, from 1933 onwards, a guard of honour was permanently mounted at the *Feldhernnhalle*. The failed attempt to overthrow the Bavarian government would be later celebrated as the sacrifice of the Alte Kämpfer, the 'old fighters' who were respected within the Party.

THE SA-SS CONFLICT

With Hitler in prison, the Party and SA forbidden and Goering exiled in Sweden after the revolt, it was left to Captain Ernst Röhm was left to carry the torch. He formed a tough paramilitary organisation in Munich, the *Frontbann*, or 'frontline battalion' with ten thousand members when Hitler came out of prison in December 1924.

It was Röhm's aim to create an official state militia intended to replace the *Reichswehr*. Hitler, still shocked at the army's lack of support during the failed Munich putsch, was initially in agreement with this. But didn't Point 22 of the Party's initial program state: *"We demand abolition of the mercenary troops* (the *Reichswehr* was a professional army) *and formation of a national army"*.

SA gathering for the Nazi Party Day
(Reichsparteitag) in Nuremberg.

3   4

Led by the *SA-Standarte* banner *'HorstWessel'*, twelve other banners parade in front of the Berlin university buildings.

For Röhm, it was obvious that the SA should progressively take over from the regular army. However, Hitler had been thinking during his spell in prison and no longer wanted to rely on a party army whose movements he had no control over.

In order to stop the dangerous expansion of the *'brown shirts'* (the distinctive emblem of the SA) after the removal of the banning of the NSDAP and SA on 30 April 1925, he placed Captain Franz Pfeffer von Salomon as their commander with the title of *Osaf* (*Oberster SA Führer*). Röhm, in disagreement with Hitler over the organisation to adopt for the SA, resigned from his position in April 1925 and left for Brazil in 1928. It was at this time that the brown shirt was adopted.

But Salomon was unable to restore order, and with the existence of grumbling against Hitler within SA ranks of certain provinces, Röhm was called back in 1930 and once again became *Sturmabteilungen* Chief-of-Staff. He too, however, failed to rein in the SA who were increasingly in the news for their bad behaviour and violence.

But, in 1925, the *Stoßtrupp* Hitler led to the creation of the 'protection squads' or *Schutzstaffeln* (SS) and from the outset, these units revealed themselves more disciplined and loyal to Hitler than the SA. Whereas the latter remained a mass working class movement, the SS were an elite whose black uniforms stood out from those of the brown shirts.

On 17 and 18 October 1931, 104,000 members of the SA, SS and even Hitler Youth children, took part in an impressive gathering at Brunswick that mocked the authorities. Thus, in December, the SA were banned by

1

the government due to the problems caused to public order. Inside the Party, Hitler, who had been given full power for a four-year period on 27 March 1933, set forth to unify all of the nationalist movements so that only one would remain, the NSDAP.

The brown army of the SA and the SS first absorbed the Stahlhelm, then the *Kyfhhaüserbund*. All of these forces were grouped together under Röhm's command. Also, all of the old Corps were integrated into Nazi organisations during a big ceremony that took place on 9 November 1933 in Munich.

After the Nazis came to power, Röhm became State Secretary, retaining his command over the Party's army. This political army comprised three million men in the spring of 1934 and had been organised, since 1932, into SA youth, marine units in some port towns, cavalry squadrons, SA air forces, motorised corps, medical units, officer and NCO schools and equipment depots placed under the responsibility of an equipment chief. Also, Röhm had formed a first reserve – *SA Reserve I* – comprising mostly former Stahlhelm members and a second reserve – *SA Reserve II* – mostly regrouping former soldiers members of the *Kyffhaüserbund*. With a strength of 300,000 prior to 30 January 1933, this number increased to 4,500,000 by the end of the year.

With the 1 December 1933 decree, the SA obtained official status and an equal footing with the army and the police, making Röhm a Reich cabinet member.

However, Röhm's ambition and the strength that he had acquired would lead to his downfall. The idea of a Germany dominated by the SA was totally unacceptable to the High Command, industry leaders hostile to socialism and the Party's SS elite.

Then, in March 1934, the *Obergruppen* and *Gruppen* commanders decided to form 'general staff guards' (*Stabswachen*) with volunteers enlisted for twelve to eighteen months. Also, contrary to strict orders issued by Hitler, these men were equipped and trained to use rifles and machine-guns.

In order to rein in the *Sturmabteilungen* that had become uncontrollable and to gain favour with the *Reichswehr* generals, Hitler decided to eliminate the SA leadership hostile to him, as well as all

1. *Sturmbannführer* of the *Pommern* Group
2. *turmführer* of the *Hessian Group*
3. *Oberstruppführer* of the *Wesrfalen Group*
4. *Scharführer* of the *Österreich* Group

those who had previously opposed him. On 30 June 1934, the SS, commanded by Himmler, and notably Sepp Dietrich's Leibstandarte Adolf Hitler, attacked by surprise and executed Röhm and those close to him in what became known as the '*Night of the long knives*'.

Then, on 13 July, Hitler declared in front of the Reichstag: '*For fourteen years I have regularly declared that the Party's combatant organisations are political institutions that have nothing to do with the army. [...] Within the State, only the army bears arms and only the National-Socialist Party holds the political power.*'

THE NEW SA

Following the violent purge, presented to the public as the elimination of men plotting to overthrow the government, thousands of SA members were eliminated, their weapons confiscated and their political power reduced to nothing.

Stripped of their exorbitant power, the SA were reduced to a junior role, especially given that their new *Stabschef*, Viktor Lutze, shone by his mediocrity and lack of character. They were reduced to appearing in official ceremonies where they represented the '*old guard*' and taking part in winter charity drives. In fact, Lutze declared, during a speech in Saxony in October 1936:

'*Our mission as SA men is to ensure that the German people remain national-socialists.*'

The removal of revolutionary ideas restored moral unity,

1. *SA-Mann* of the *Motorsturm* of the *Berlin-Brandenburg* Group
2. *Doctor (Sturmbannführer)* of the *Schlesien* Group
3. *SA-Mann* of the *Südwest Group*
4. Treasurer-paymaster *(Oberrechnungsführer)* of the *Westmark* Group

DISTRIBUTION AND ORIGIN OF SA STRENGTH IN 1933	
• Original SA, including SS	300 000
• First intake of *Stahlhem* members	550 000
• Second intake of *Stahlhem* members	450 000
• Integration of the *Kyffhaüserbund*	1 500 000
• *Reiter-SA*, cavalrymen from rural horse riding clubs	200 000
• *Marine-SA*, former nautical club members	50 000
• Border defence units	100 000
• Technische Nothilfe engineers	50 000
• Red Cross and charitable association members	60 000
• University and technical college students	100 000
• Secondary school pupils	150 000
• Brigade Ehrardt	150 000
• Oberland flying club	200 000
• Civil servants	200 000
• *Ehrenführer*, SA honour members	20 000
• Uniformed detachments of various right-wing parties, notably the *Reichsbanner*	420 000

and the subordination to the *Reichswehr* restored homogeneity. The organisation set up by Röhm remained, however. The SA were not submitted to local control but came under the command of the Party (*Reichsleitung der NSDAP*). The High Command remained in Munich, 'the capital of the Nazi movement', even though several offices were set up in Berlin.

The importance of the SA then became more military than political as their presence allowed Hitler and the generals to conceal the growing strength of the army. Thus, with the introduction of military service in 1935, the *Reichswehr* concentrated on the systematic military training of 200,000 specially selected SA who served in their own uniform. Training regiments *(Lehr-Regimenter)*

Recruits of *Motorstandarte 30 'Enst von Rath' NSKK* take their oath of loyalty.

were formed in several camps with military leadership for a three-month training period.

After the adoption of military service, the SA were called up in the normal manner and during their service, they ceased all political activity.

Active service SA, aged between 18 and 35, were particularly affected by the purge. Their strength fell from 1,000,000 to 500,000, notably due to being split into three independent organisations (*Sturmabteilungen, Schutzstaffeln and Nationalsozialistisches Kraftfahrkorps*) of which each commander was under the direct orders of the Führer.

After the disbanding of the original *Obergruppen*, the SA comprised twenty-one *Gruppen* divided into one hundred and twenty Brigaden subdivided into more than five hundred

3 4

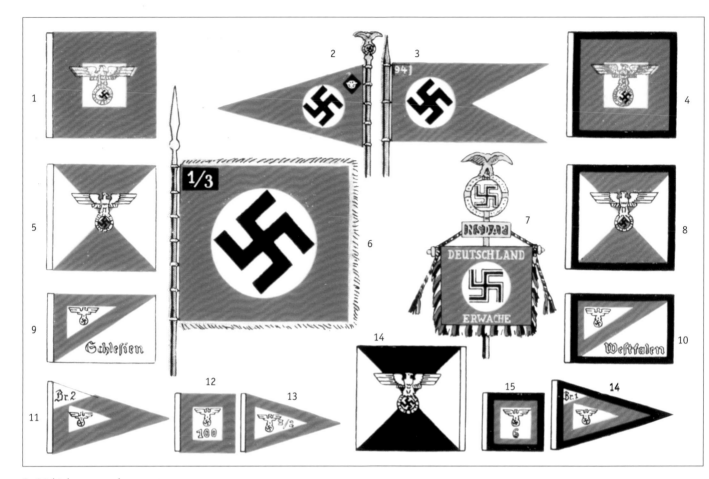

1. SA high command pennant
2. *Motorsturm* pennant
3. *Reitersturm* pennant
4. Chief of motorised units pennant
5. *Obergruppe* pennant
6. *Sturm SA* flag
7. xxxxxxxxxxx
8. *Obergruppen* sign
9. *Gruppen* pennant
10. *Gruppen* sign
11. *Brigade* pennant
12. *Standarte* pennant
13. *Sturmbann* pennant
14. *SS-Reichsführung* pennant
15. *Staffelstab*
16. *Oberstaffelstab*

• Bayerische Ostmark	Eastern Bavaria	Bayreuth
• Berlin-Brandenburg	Berlin-Brandenburg	Berlin
• Franken	Franconia	Nuremberg
• Hansa	Hansa	Hamburg
• Hessen	Hessen	Kassel
• Hochland	Highlands	Munich
• Kurpfalz	Palatinat	Mannheim
• Mitte	Centre	Magdeburg
• Mittelrhein	Rhineland	Coblence
• Niederrhein	Lower Rhineland	Dusseldorf
• Niedersachsen	Lower Saxony	Hanover
• Nordmark	Northern territories	Kiel
• Nordsee	Nordsee	Bremen
• Ostland	East Land	Königsberg
• Pommern	Vorpommern	Stettin
• Sachsen	Saxony	Dresden
• Schlesien	Silesia	Breslau
• Südwest	South West	Stuttgart
• Thüringen	Thüringen	Weimar
• Warthe	Warta	Posen
• Westfalen	Westphalia	Haltern

The choice of names was quite deliberate and aimed at erasing the structures inherited from the past, such as Baden, Württemberg or Bavaria.

Standarten or regiments, some of which were cavalry. Under SA command were *SA-Gruppen* (divisions) comprising 15 to 25,000 men bearing a geographical or regional name. They comprised two to seven *SA-Brigaden*, and between two to six thousand men, designated by an Arabic numeral. On average, each brigade controlled, four *Standarten* (regiments), one of which was cavalry and sometimes one naval. The next lower echelon was the *Sturmbann* (battalion) and the *Sturm* (company) which was the lowest unit to have a permanent command post and was organised into *Trupps* (platoons) and *Scharen* (groups).

In 1933, each *Gruppe* formed a battalion HQ comprising full-time professionals, equipped on army lines. Known as Sturmbann z.b.V., these units were tasked with assisting the police. The same year saw the formation of the *SA-Verfügungstruppen* who, since the Treaty of Versailles had authorised the arming of postal and railway security personnel, were attached to and partially incorporated into, the *Postschutz* and the *Bahnschutz*.

The SAR I comprised men aged between 35 and 45 who, due to being mostly armed forces, saw their training. There were twenty-one brigades (one per active *Gruppe*) divided into Standarten.

The SAR II comprised men over 45 years of age who remained grouped together in veteran associations.

NAZI PARTY FORMATIONS

If 1933 was the year of rapid SA expansion, 1934 was the year of its decline. The SS, however, became increasingly powerful, whereas the SA was progressively stripped of all the components that Röhm had added to it. The SS and the *NSKK* became independent, the Ehrardt Brigade was integrated into the SA, the *Kyffhaüserbund* continued helping veterans and the Flieger-SA, formed with the personnel of the numerous private flying clubs and the incorporation of the Oberland, joined the German association for aerial sports that had recently been created by Goering in order to secretly promote the future Luftwaffe.

1. Drum Major of the Westmark Group.
2. Musician *Rottenführer* of the Schlesien Group.
3. *SA-Mann* of the Thüringen Group.
4. *Marinesturm*.

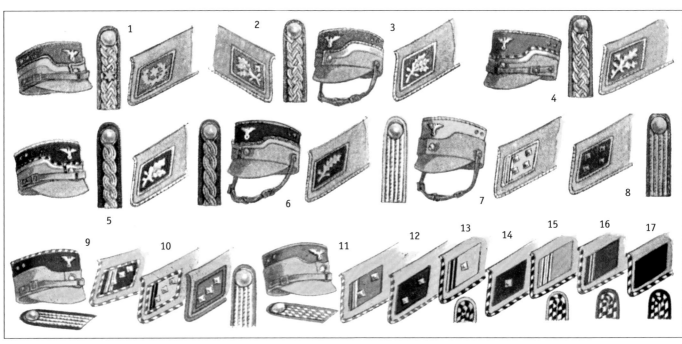

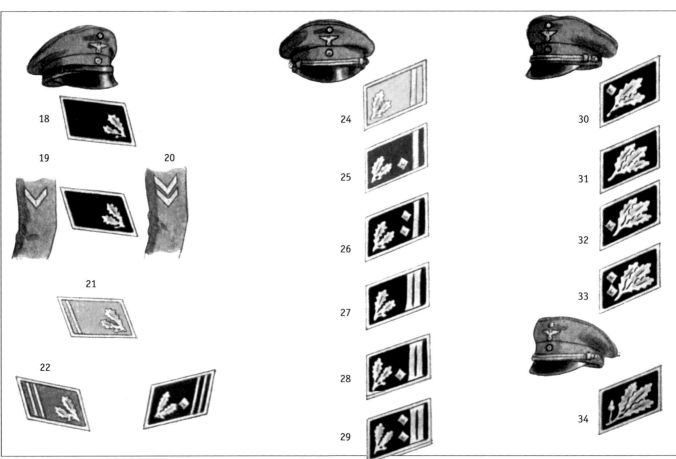

35   36   37   38

SS recruits take the oath of loyalty on their battalion emblem.

Then, in 1936, the *Nationalsozialistisches Reiterkorps* (NSRK) became autonomous, with its commander still under SA control, technically speaking,

DIE SCHUTZSTAFFELN

The SS, who had carried out the executions during the 30 June repression, obviously emerged as

1. SS-Gruppenführer in greatcoat
2. SS-Obersturmbannführer (Schlesien)
3. SS-Sturmann musician
4. SS-Mann

1

2

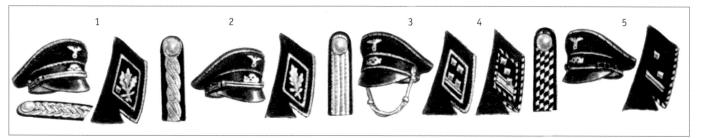

the victors of the confrontation with the SA to whom they no longer had to take any orders.

Under Hitler's direct control, they were an elite unit comprising men aged between 18 and 24, rigorously selected according to moral, ideological and physical factors. The minimum height requirement was 1 m 70 and they were totally dedicated to the Führer.

SS strength grew from 220,000 to 300,000 men. Their

Headdress, shoulder straps and collar tabs
1. From *Reichsführer der SS* to *SS-Brigadeführer*
2. *SS-Oberführer* and *SS-Standartenführer*
3. and 4. From *SS-Obersturmbannführer* to *SS-Sturmführer*
5. From *SS-Obertruppführer* to *SS-Mann*

role was defined by their commander, Himmler, in his 1 January 1934 order of the day:

'To find, fight and destroy all known or unknown enemies of the Führer, the national-socialist movement and the resurrection of the race. By carrying out this mission, we will not spare our blood, nor that of foreigners if the Fatherland demands it.'

Stationed in barracks, they were a permanent force tasked with protecting Hitler and the main figures of the Nazi Party, whilst at the same time forming political police detachments.

SS-Schutzstaffeln officers and NCOs leave a meeting.

SS-Obergruppenfürher Sepp Dietrich at a parade of a *Heer* artillery formation.

The SS were formed into ten *Oberabschnitte* divided into thirty *Abschnitte* subdivided into one hundred and ten *Standarte*: twenty motorised, ten cavalry, eight on foot. Perfectly equipped (especially in armament), they were the thorn in the side of the *Reichswehr*. There was a prospect, at the beginning of 1935, of reaching a compromise, with only the personal guards retaining their weapons and part of the rest of the SS personnel being incorporated into the *Reichswehr* in the shape of an SS division!

DIE HITLERJUGEND

13 May 1922 saw the creation, within the SA, of the *Jugendbund der NSDAP*. Its beginnings were marked by confusion caused by their uniform, identical to that of the SA, and by the aggressiveness of its older members.

In 1933, the 'Hitler Youth' (*Hitlerjugend or HJ*) officially became independent. Scout organisations were forbidden, and all the clubs and youth organisations were incorporated into the HJ. Baldur von Schirach, president of the Nazi student association, was placed as their leader. Recruitment was initially on a voluntary basis.

The aim of the HJ leadership was to raise and educate German youth in the spirit of national-socialism, not only in body, but also on a spiritual and moral level. This was the expression of the will and the future of young generations. This concerned boys aged between 10 and 18 and soon, girls aged between 10 and 21.

The HJ was organised into:

• *Kameradschaft* with ten boys, tasked with forging the indestructible unity of its members.

• *Schar* comprising four to five *Kameradschaften*.

• *Gefolgschaft* made up of four *Scharen* thus forming the smallest unit.

• *Stamm* regrouping three to five Gefolgschaften, depen-

Adolf Hitler *and SS-Reichsführer*
Heinrich Himmler.

1. *Gebietsführer*
2. *Bannführer*
3. *Scharführer*
4. *Kameradschaftführer*

ding on the population of the region in question.
  • *Bann* comprising four to eight Stämme corresponding to a borough (Kreis).
  • *Gebiet* grouping ten to forty Banne and corresponding to a region (Gau).
    The League of German Maidens (*Mädelbund in der Hitlerjugend* or BDM) was organised along the same lines as the boys.

DAS NATIONALSOZIALISTISCHEN KRAFTFAHR-KORPS

The NSKK was the former automobile unit of the brown shirt army. It was now formed by the merger of the old automobile corps and the numerous motorised formations that had been taken from the SA.

On 1 April 1930, the Nazionalsozialistischen *Automobil Korps* (NSAK) was created by Franz von Pfeffer who recruited within the ranks of the SA all men with an interest in cars or motorbikes in order to ensure mobility for

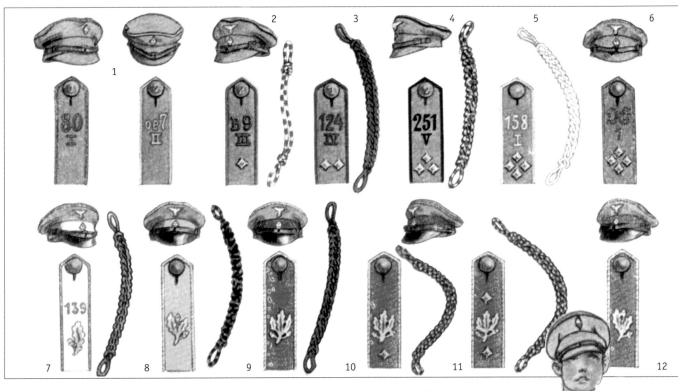

the Party. This was indispensable to its struggle for power given that the main strength of Hitler's militias lay in their tenacity and mobility.

At the end of the year, von Pfeffer having made way for Hühlein, the NSAK was reorganised into *Motorstandarten*, *Motorstaffeln* and *Motorstürme*. It was given the name of NSKK on 1 May 1931.

Another group, the *Motor-SA* (MSA) was formed on 15 May 1931 from the Munich detachment equipped with trucks purchased after 1922 for transporting local shock troops.

After 30 June 1934, the NSKK became independent and was placed directly under the Führer's orders. Four months later, it merged with the MSA. Its manpower now stood at 350,000 members and it was organised into twenty-one brigades, each corresponding to a *SA Gruppe*, divided into *Abteilungen* for transport units and Motor Standarten for the former MSA.

DER NS-ARBEITS-DIENST

1931 saw the creation of the *NS-Freiwillige Arbeitsdienst* intended to fight unemployment. The government of Chancellor Brüning then authorised work camps and the NSDAP organised its own camps. Then, on 26 June 1935, work became obligatory and the NSDAP became a state organisation. From this date

1. *Hitler-Junge (Österreich)*
2. *Kameradschaftführer (Bayern)*. The cord here is in the colour of the province, whereas in the rest of the Reich it was in the colour seen in the illustrations.
3. *Scharführer*
4. *Gefolgschaftsführer*
5. and 6. *Unterbannführer* serving in an *Obergebiet Staff*.
7. *Bannführer*
8. *Oberbannführer*
9. *Gebietsführer*
10. *Obergebietsführer*
11. *Stabsführer*
12. *Oberbannführer* serving in a *Staff*.

1. Hitler Youth with drum
2. *Jungbannführer des deutschen Jungvolks in der HJ*
3. *Jungvolljunge*
4. *Jungvolljunge*

Obergruppenführer Karl Sauke, *NSFK* Chief-of-Staff, solemnly awards a prize to one of the winners of a competition organised by the corps. *(ECPA)*

onwards, all young people aged between 17 and 25 had to, before being called up for the army, serve six months in the *Reichsarbeitsdienst*. The RAD continued to be part of the Party, and its chief (*Reichsarbeitsführer*) was named as a party executive member (*Reichsleiter*).

With 400,000 members at the beginning of 1935, it was organised into thirty work regions (*Arbeitsgaue*) divided into groups subdivided into 215-man detachments spread among

89

TENO officer (*TN-Bereitschaftführer*)
and NCO.
(ECPA)

several camps when necessary. The
leadership generally comprised former
military personnel, and the workers regularly took part in very military exercises: troop school, individual combat
training, day and night route marches,
rifle range, basic signals training.

FORMATIONS UNDER NSDAP PATRONAGE

During the course of 1933-1934,
several organisations changed status,
going from Party to state and vice-ver-
sa or disappearing whilst others were
created.

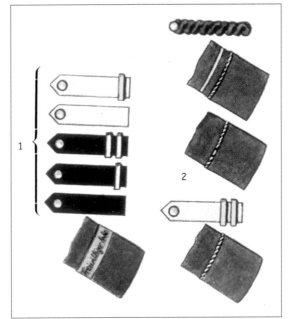

DER REICHSLUFTSCHUTZBUND

After being disbanded by Hermann Goering on 29 April 1933 due to the creation of the Luftwaffe, a new civil defence organisation was formed in order to convince the German population of the vital importance of air raid protection and to gain active cooperation.

The *Reichsluftschutzbund* began in the domain of propaganda directed at the population via a specialist magazine named *Die Sirene* and a few booklets explaining what to do in the event of an air raid, the first thing being the carrying of a gas mask. This information was completed by talks given in schools by RLB members. A law promulgated on 16 March 1935 stipulated that all Germans had to take part in RLB service. Any person residing in Germany could be requisitioned for police service with the RLB. Finally, a decree dated 26 June, applicable on 1 July, gave the Air Minster control over air raid defence, but the RLB was not disbanded. The

Labour service flags parade in Nuremberg during the Party day.

latter was finally a civil organisation with a president at its head, under Air Ministry and *Luftwaffe* Commander-in-Chief control. Its role consisted of:

— ensuring that civilians knew what to do in the event of air raids

— training its members in civil defence.

It was organised into groups (*Gruppen*), district groups (*Bezirksgruppen*), local groups (*Ortsgruppen*), neighbourhood groups (*Reviergruppen*) or communal groups (*Gemeindegruppen*), sub-groups (*Untergruppen*) and Blocks.

DIE TECHNISCHE NOTHILFE

Like the RLB, the 'technical emergency help' was a civil organisation

Technische Nothilfe
1. *Nothelfer, Gruppenführer, Truppführer, Zugführer* and *Abteilungsführer.*
2. *Führer des Dienstes*
3. Provincial command representative
4. Nothelfer of the technical service
5. Voluntary labour service chief
6. Civil defence group leader

4

5

6

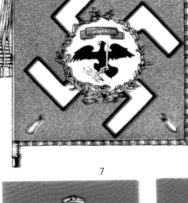

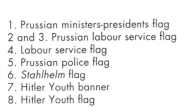

1. Prussian ministers-presidents flag
2 and 3. Prussian labour service flag
4. Labour service flag
5. Prussian police flag
6. *Stahlhelm* flag
7. Hitler Youth banner
8. Hitler Youth flag

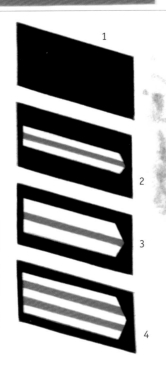

Adolf Hitler presents flags to *NS-Fliegerkorps* units, the very last organisation to depend on the Party.

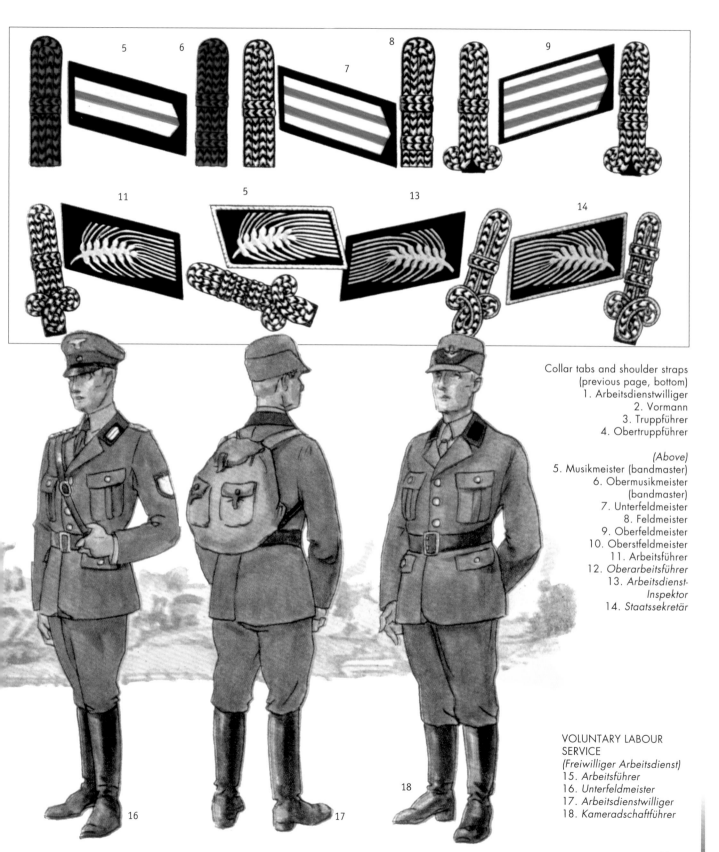

Collar tabs and shoulder straps
(previous page, bottom)
1. Arbeitsdienstwilliger
2. Vormann
3. Truppführer
4. Obertruppführer

(Above)
5. Musikmeister (bandmaster)
6. Obermusikmeister
(bandmaster)
7. Unterfeldmeister
8. Feldmeister
9. Oberfeldmeister
10. Oberstfeldmeister
11. Arbeitsführer
12. Oberarbeitsführer
13. Arbeitsdienst-
Inspektor
14. Staatssekretär

VOLUNTARY LABOUR
SERVICE
(Freiwilliger Arbeitsdienst)
15. Arbeitsführer
16. Unterfeldmeister
17. Arbeitsdienstwilliger
18. Kameradschaftführer

The first four banners (*Feldzeichen*, a sort of terrain rallying emblem) are presented to the SA on the Marschfeld in Munich on 27 January 1923.

Oberforstmeister, right, photographed during a meeting in Berlin in 1934.

organised into regional groups (*Landesgruppen*), subdivided into local groups (*Ortsgruppen*).

Its origins went back to a technical service of the Garde-Kavallerie-Schützendivision comprising experienced sappers that had decided to '*loyally preserve the spirit of their arm until better times*'.

Created in 1919 by the government of the Weimar Republic, the *Technische Nothilfe* was a strike-breaking organisation tasked with maintaining vital infrastructure. In the years with fewer strikes, the Teno was mostly used as a technical reserve in the event of a natural disaster. After 1933, it was reorganised into a national formation.

THE ADMINISTRATIONS CAME UNDER
REICH & LÄNDER CONTROL

In imperial or republican Germany, many people wore military style clothing. This increased when the national-socialists took power advocating *'total war'* and, therefore, the participation of the entire population, to such an extent that soon, virtually everyone wore a uniform of some kind.

Among of the organisations that were military in character were the German Red Cross, Customs, Railways, Post and river and forest authorities.

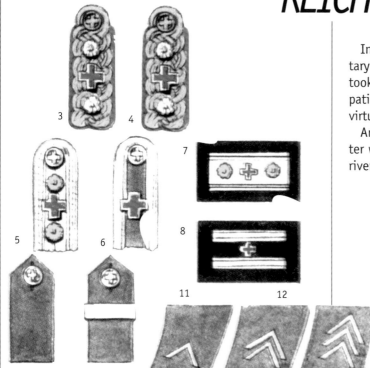

THE GERMAN RED CROSS (*DAS DEUTSCHE ROTEKREUZ* OR DRK)
1. *Vorsitzender der Sanitätskolonne* (medical group vice-president)
2. *Zugführer-Stellvertreter* (deputy section chief)
3. *Präsident des DRK und Stellvertreter* (president of the DRK and his deputy)
4. *Vorsitzender der Landesvereine und Stellvertreter* (vice-president of provincial associations and his deputy)
Abteilungsvorsitzender der Landesvereine (vice-president of the detachment of provincial associations and his deputy): with a rosette
Mitglied der Landesvereine (member of provincial associations): without rosette
Nota: The base colour was grey in provincial associations.
5. *Vorsitzender der Sanitätskolonne usw.* (vice-president of the medical column, etc.)
Kolonnenführer (group leader): with rosette
Kolonnenführer-Stellvertreter (group leader deputy): without rosette
6. *Schriftführer* (secretary), *Kassenführer* (cashier), *Zeugwart* (storeman).
7. *Vorsitzender der Sanitätskolonne* – armlet worn on civilian clothing
8. *Schriftführer usw.* (secretary, etc.) – armband worn on civilian clothing
9. *Mitglieder der Sanitätskolonne* (members of the medical group)
10. *Mitglieder der Sanitätskolonne mit bestandener Zug- und Gruppenführerprüfung* (members of medical groups), with control of sections and groups
11. *Gruppenführer* (group leader)
12. *Zugführer-Stellvertreter* (section leader deputy)
13. *Zugführer* (section leader)

CUSTOMS
(*ZOLLWESEN*)
1. *Oberzollrat* (chief customs advisor) wearing the tunic with a double row of buttons.
2. *Zollamtmann* (customs officer with the customs administration) wearing the tunic with a single row of buttons.
3. *Oberzollmaschinist* (customs chief mechanic)
4. *Zollpraktikant* (customs trainee) in greatcoat

THE RAILWAYS
(*REISCHBHANN*)
COLLAR TABS
1. Pay level n° 1
2. Pay level n° 2
4. Pay level n° 3 (station employee)
5. Pay level n° 4
6. Pay level n° 5 (train chief)
7. Pay level n° 6 (locomotive driver)
8. Pay level n° 7
9. Pay level n° 8
10. Pay level n° 9

SLEEVE INSIGNIA
(high seas, inland waters and coastline)
12. Pay level n° 3
13. Pay level n° 4
18. Pay level n° 5
19. Pay level n ° 6
16. Pay level n° 7

17. Pay level n° 8

HEADDRESS
3. Service cap
14. Pay levels n° 3 and 4 (high seas, inland waters and coastline)
15. Pay levels n° 5 to 8 (ditto)
20. *Beamter der Befoldungsgruppe VIII* (pay level n° 8 civil servant) with greatcoat
21. *Beamter der Befoldungsgruppe V* (pay level n° 5 civil servant) station surveillance with the tunic with two rows of buttons
23. *Beamter der Befoldungsgruppe III* (pay level n° 3 civil service) with the tunic with a single row of buttons
23. *Beamter der Befoldungsgruppe III* attached to high seas service

POSTAL SERVICE (REICHSPOST)
Collar tabs
1. Auxiliary controller
2. Postman
3. Auxiliary automobile driver
4. Automobile driver
5. Controller
6. Chief controller and operating assistant
7. Trainee
8. Assistant
9. Secretary
10. Qualified chief secretary
11. Unclassified employee
12. Trainee
13. Chief secretary
14. Inspector
15. Chief inspector
16. Category A civil servant
17. Category A civil servant in a decision making post
18. Postman
19. Postal secretary
20. Postman with the three-quarter length coat and Baschlik cap
21. Postal secretary with coat

RIVERS AND FORESTRY (*FORSTWESEN*)
Parade uniform (Prussia)
1. *Oberlandforstmeister* in parade uniform (Prussia)
2. *Landforstmeister* in parade uniform
3. *Revierförster* in parade uniform (district forestry guard)
4. *Revierförster* in parade uniform

Drawings by Knötel from the German manual "Uniformfibel 1933". Private Collection, All Rights Reserved.

Design and layout by Jean-Marie Mongin
© *Histoire & Collections* 2013

ISBN: 978-2-35250-281-4
Publisher's number: 35250

© Histoire & Collections 2013

Book edited by
HISTOIRE & COLLECTIONS
5, avenue de la République
F-75541 Paris Cedex 11 - FRANCE
Tel: +33 (0) 1 40 21 18 20
Fax: +33 (0) 1 47 00 51 11
www.histoireetcollections.com

This book has been designed, typed, laid-out
and processed by Histoire & Collections
on fully integrated computer equipment.

Color separation: Studio H&C
Print by Calidad Grafica
Spain, European Union,
April 2013